FAIRY TALES
AND
CHILDREN

FAIRY TALES and CHILDREN

The Psychology of Children Revealed through Four of Grimm's Fairy Tales

CARL-HEINZ MALLET

Translated by Joachim Neugroschel

SCHOCKEN BOOKS • NEW YORK

First American edition published by Schocken Books 1984
10 9 8 7 6 5 4 3 2 1   84 85 86 87
Copyright © 1984 Schocken Books Inc.
All rights reserved
Title of original German edition: *Kennen Sie Kinder?*
Copyright © 1980 by Hoffmann und Campe Verlag, Hamburg

Library of Congress Cataloging in Publication Data
Mallet, Carl-Heinz, 1926 –
Fairy tales and children.
Translation of: Kennen Sie Kinder?
Bibliography: p.
1. Kinder- und Hausmächen. 2. Children's stories—Psychological aspects. I.
Title.
PT921.M3213 1984 398.2′1′0943 83–40464

Design by Nancy Dale Muldoon
Manufactured in the United States of America
ISBN 0-8052-3897-2

Contents

THE FAIRY TALES

Hansel and Gretel

O UTSIDE a large forest, there lived a poor woodcutter with his wife and his two children. The little boy was named Hansel and the little girl Gretel. The woodcutter had almost nothing to eat, and once, when a great famine came into the land, he could no longer earn their daily bread. In bed at night, he was so nervous and so worried that he tossed and turned. With a sigh, he said to his wife, "What's to become of us? How can we feed our poor children if we don't even have enough for ourselves?"

"Do you know what, husband?" answered the wife. "Early tomorrow morning, we will take the children out to the densest part of the forest. We will light a fire for them there and give each of them a piece of bread. Then we will go about our work and leave them alone. They will not find the way home again, and we will be rid of them."

"No, wife," said the husband, "I will not do it. How can I have the heart to leave my children alone in the forest? The wild beasts would soon come and tear them to shreds."

"Oh, you fool," she said, "then all four of us will starve to death. All you can do is plane the boards for the coffins." And she gave him no peace until he agreed.

These fairy tales are translations from Grimm.

3

"But I feel so sorry for the poor children," said the husband. The two children had been too hungry to fall asleep. And they had heard what their stepmother said to their father. Gretel wept bitter tears and said to Hansel, "Now we are doomed."

"Quiet, Gretel," said Hans, "do not fret. I will figure something out." And when the parents had gone to sleep, he got up, put on his little coat, opened the lower part of the Dutch door, and stole outside. The moon was shining very brightly, and the white pebbles lying in front of the house gleamed like silver coins. Hansel bent down and stuffed as many of the pebbles into his jacket pocket as it could hold. Then he went back and said to Gretel, "Everything is all right, dear little sister, you can sleep peacefully. God will not abandon us." And he lay down in his bed again.

When day broke, the wife came before the sun had even risen and woke the two children. "Get up, you lazybones, we are going into the forest to fetch wood." Then she gave each of them a piece of bread and said, "Here is something for lunch, but do not eat it up. This is all you are getting."

Gretel took the bread and put it under her apron, because Hansel had the stones in his pocket. Then they all set out toward the forest.

After walking for a short while, Hansel stood still and peered back at the house, and he kept doing this over and over again.

The father said, "Hansel, why do you keep looking back and lagging behind? Pay attention and keep walking."

"Oh, Father," said Hansel, "I am looking at my white kitten sitting up on the roof. It wants to say goodbye to me."

The wife said, "Fool, that is not your kitten, that is the morning sun shining on the chimney." But Hansel had not seen the kitten. He had been throwing the shiny pebbles from his pocket to the road.

When they reached the middle of the forest, the father said, "Now gather wood, children. I want to start a fire so that you will not be cold."

Hansel and Gretel collected twigs, building a small mound.

The twigs were lit, and when the flame was blazing nicely, the wife said, "Now lie down by the fire, children, and have a rest. We are going into the forest to chop wood. When we are finished, we will come back for you."

Hansel and Gretel sat by the fire, and when it was noon, each ate a piece of bread. And because they heard the strokes of the ax, they believed that their father was nearby. But it was not the ax, it was a branch that he had tied to a withered tree and that the wind was beating to and fro. And when the children had been sitting like that for a long time, they became so tired that they could not keep their eyes open, and they fell sound asleep.

By the time they awoke, it was the dead of night. Gretel began to weep and said, "How are we to get out of the forest!"

But Hansel comforted her. "Just wait a bit until the moon has risen. Then we are sure to find the way."

And when the full moon was up, Hansel took his little sister by the hand and followed the pebbles. They shimmered like freshly minted silver coins and showed them the way. The children walked all night and came to their father's house again just as day was breaking. They knocked at the door, and when the wife opened and saw that it was Hansel and Gretel, she said, "You wicked children, why did you sleep in the forest so long? We thought you did not want to come back."

But the father was delighted, for it had grieved him deeply that he had left them all alone.

Not long after that, there was famine again everywhere, and the children heard the mother say to the father in bed at night, "Everything has been eaten up again. All we have left is half a loaf of bread—then it will be all over for us. The children will have to leave. We will take them deeper into the forest so that they will not find the way back to us again. Otherwise, there is no hope for us."

The man's heart was heavy, and he thought, "It would be better if you shared the last morsel with your children." But the wife would not listen to anything he said. She scolded him and reproached him. If you are in for a penny, you are in for a pound, and since he had given in the first time, he had to give in the second time as well.

However, the children had still been awake and had eavesdropped on the conversation. When the parents were asleep, Hansel got up again to go outside and gather pebbles like the last time. But the wife had locked the door, and Hansel could not get out. Still, he comforted his little sister, saying, "Do not cry, Gretel, and sleep peacefully. The good Lord will help us."

Early in the morning, the wife came and got the children out of bed. They each received a piece of bread, but it was smaller than the last time. On the way to the forest, Hansel crumbled his bread in his pocket, often stopping to throw a crumb on the ground.

"Hansel, why are you standing there looking back?" said the father. "Keep going."

"I am looking back at my little dove. It is sitting on the roof and wants to say goodbye to me," replied Hansel.

"Fool," said the wife, "that is not your little dove. It is the morning sun shining on the chimney." But Hansel threw all the crumbs on the road, one by one.

The wife led the children much deeper into the forest, where they had never been before in their lives. Once again, a large fire was lit, and the mother said, "Just stay seated here, children, and when you are tired, you can sleep a little. We are going into the forest to chop wood, and in the evening, when we are done, we will come back for you."

When it was noon, Gretel shared her bread with Hansel, who had strewn his bread along the way. Then they fell asleep, and the evening passed, but no one came to the poor children. They did not awake until the dead of night. Hansel comforted his little sister and said, "Just wait, Gretel, until the moon comes up. Then we will see the bread crumbs that I have strewn. They will show us the way home."

When the moon came up, they set out, but they did not find the bread crumbs, for the many thousands of birds that fly about in the woods and fields had pecked them up.

Hansel said to Gretel, "We will find the way, do not worry."

But they did not find it. They walked all night and then all day from morning to evening, but they did not come out of the forest, and they were so hungry, for they had nothing but a few berries that were on the ground. And because they were so tired that their legs could not carry them any farther, they lay down under a tree and fell asleep.

By now, it was the third morning since they had left their father's house. They began walking again, but they kept getting deeper and deeper into the forest, and if help did not come soon, they were certain to perish. When it was noon, they saw a lovely snow-white bird perched on a branch. It sang so beautifully that they stopped and listened to it. And when it was done, it flapped its wings and flew in front of them, and they followed it, until they reached a cottage. The bird alighted on the roof, and when they came very near, they saw that the cottage was made of bread and the roof of cake. The windows, however, were of white sugar.

"Let us start in and have a fine feast," said Hansel. "I will eat a piece of the roof, Gretel, and you can eat from the window. It tastes sweet."

Hansel reached up and broke off a bit of the roof to see what it tasted like, and Gretel stood at the panes and nibbled on them. Suddenly, a fine voice called from inside:

> *Nibble, munch, and crunch!*
> *Who's eating my house for lunch?*

The children answered:

> *The wind so mild,*
> *The heavenly child.*

And they kept on eating, unabashed. Hansel, who found the roof very tasty, tore off a large chunk, and Gretel pushed out a whole round window pane, sat down, and ate heartily.

All at once the door opened, and a very old woman came

creeping out, leaning on a crutch. Hansel and Gretel were so frightened that they dropped whatever they were holding in their hands. But the old woman shook her head and said, "Oh, you dear children, who has brought you here? Just come in and stay with me. No harm will come to you." She took each one by the hand and led them into her cottage. Good food was served— milk and pancakes with sugar, apples, and nuts. Then Hansel and Gretel lay down on two lovely little beds covered in white, and felt as if they were in heaven.

The old woman was only pretending to be friendly, however. She was really a wicked witch who lay in wait for children, and she had built the bread cottage only to lure them. Whenever she got a child in her clutches, she would kill it, boil it, and eat it, and that was a holiday for her. Witches have red eyes and cannot see very far, but they have a fine sense of smell, like animals, and they can tell when people are approaching. When Hansel and Gretel drew near, she had laughed and said scornfully, "I've got them now. They won't get away from me."

Early in the morning, before the children awoke, she got up, and when she saw the two of them sleeping so sweetly, with their full, red cheeks, she murmured to herself, "They'll make a tasty morsel."

Then she grabbed Hansel with her bony hand and carried him into a small stable and locked him up behind a barred gate. He could scream all he liked; it was no use.

Then she went to Gretel, shook her awake, and shouted, "Get up, lazybones. Fetch water and cook something nice for your brother. He is outside in the stable, and he has to fatten up. When he is fat, I will eat him." Gretel began to weep bitterly, but it was no use, she had to do what the wicked witch demanded.

Now, the best food was cooked for poor Hansel, but Gretel was given nothing but crab shells. Every morning the old woman stole out to the little stable and cried, "Hansel, stick out your finger so that I can feel whether you will soon be fat." But Hansel stuck out a small bone, and the old woman, who had weak eyes, could not see it and thought it was Hansel's finger, and she was surprised that he was not fattening up.

When four weeks had gone by and Hansel was still skinny, the witch lost patience, and she would not wait any longer.

"Hey, Gretel," she shouted at the girl, "step lively and fetch water. Hansel may be fat or skinny, but tomorrow I will slaughter him and boil him."

Oh, how the poor little girl wailed when she had to fetch the water, and how the tears rolled down her cheeks! "Dear God, please help us," she cried. "If only the wild beasts had eaten us in the forest, then we would at least have died together."

"Stop blubbering," said the old woman. "It won't help."

Early in the morning, Gretel had to get out of bed in order to hang up the caldron of water and light the fire. "First we will do the baking," said the old woman. "I have already started the oven and kneaded the dough." She pushed poor Gretel outside to the oven, from which the flames were already leaping forth. "Crawl in," said the witch, "and see whether it is hot enough so that we can put the bread in."

The witch intended to close the oven door when Gretel was inside, so that Gretel would roast, and then the witch would eat her up. But Gretel realized what the witch had in mind, and she said, "I don't know how to do it. How do I get inside?"

"You silly goose," said the old woman. "The opening is large enough, as you can see—I could get in myself." She crept over and stuck her head inside the oven. Gretel gave her such a hard push that the witch fell in very far. Then Gretel closed the iron door and bolted it. Ooh, now the old woman began to howl, so terribly. But Gretel ran away, and the godless witch had to burn up miserably.

Gretel ran straight to the little stable, opened it, and cried, "Hansel, we are saved! The old witch is dead!" Hansel sprang out like a bird from a cage when the door opened. How happy they were—they hugged, jumped around, and kissed! And because they no longer had to be afraid, they went into the witch's house. Here, chests of pearls and precious stones were lying in all nooks and crannies.

"These are better than pebbles," said Hansel and stuffed his pockets until they were full.

And Gretel said, "I want to take something home, too," and she filled up her apron.

"But now we have to go," said Hansel, "so that we can get out of the witch's forest."

After walking for several hours, they came to a large body of water. "We cannot get across," said Hansel. "I do not see a plank or a bridge."

"And no boats sail here," replied Gretel. "But a white duck is swimming over there. If I ask her, she will help us across." And she called:

> *Little duck, little duck,*
> *Hansel and Gretel are standing here,*
> *Without a plank or bridge.*
> *Take us on your white back.*

The little duck swam over, and Hansel sat down on it and invited his little sister to sit down next to him.

"No," replied Gretel. "The two of us will be too heavy for the little duck. Let her carry each of us in turn."

The good little creature did so, and when the children had been brought across safe and sound and had then walked for a while, the forest began to look more and more familiar, and finally they saw their father's house from afar. They began to run. They dashed into the house and threw their arms around their father. The man had not had a happy hour since he had left the children in the forest. However, his wife had died. Gretel emptied out her apron so that the pearls and precious stones jumped around the room, and Hansel threw one handful after another out of his pocket. All their worries were over, and they lived together in great joy.

My tale is told, a mouse runs bold, whoever catches it can make a fur cap out of it.

Little Red Riding Hood

ONCE upon a time there was a sweet little girl. Anyone who so much as looked at her loved her, and the person who loved her most was her grandmother, who could not stop giving gifts to the child. Once, the grandmother gave her a riding hood of red velvet, and because the child looked so good in it and would not wear anything else, she was known only as Little Red Riding Hood.

One day her mother said to her, "Come, Little Red Riding Hood, here is a piece of cake and a bottle of wine. Take them out to Grandmother. She is sick and weak, and she will enjoy them. Start out before it gets hot, and when you are out, walk decently and do not leave the path, or you will fall and break the glass, and Grandmother has nothing. And when you enter her home, do not forget to say good morning, and do not look around in all the corners."

"I will do everything correctly," Little Red Riding Hood said to her mother and gave her her hand upon it. However, the Grandmother lived out in the woods, half an hour from the village. And when Little Red Riding Hood came into the forest, she encountered the wolf. Little Red Riding Hood did not know what a wicked animal he was, and she was not afraid of him.

"Good day, Little Red Riding Hood," he said.

"Thank you, Wolf."

"Where are you off to so early, Little Red Riding Hood?"

"To Grandmother's house."

"What are you carrying under your apron?"

"Cake and wine. We did our baking yesterday. My sick, weak Grandmother will enjoy some of it and grow stronger."

"Little Red Riding Hood, where does your grandmother live?"

"A good fifteen minutes farther into the woods. Her house is under the three big oak trees. The nut hedges are below. You must know that," said Little Red Riding Hood.

The wolf thought to himself, "This tender young thing is a juicy morsel. She will taste even better than the old woman. I'll have to use cunning if I want to grab both of them."

He walked alongside Little Red Riding Hood for a while. Then he said, "Little Red Riding Hood, just look at the beautiful flowers growing all about. Why not have a look around? I believe you don't even hear the little birds singing so sweetly. You walk along as if you were going to school, and it is so delightful out in the woods."

Little Red Riding Hood opened her eyes wide, and when she saw the rays of sunshine dancing to and fro among the trees and all the beautiful flowers, she thought, "If I bring Grandmother a fresh bouquet, it will make her feel good. It is so early in the day that I am sure to arrive on time." So she ran off the road and into the forest and looked for flowers. And whenever she picked one, she thought there was a more beautiful flower farther out, and she ran after it, and she kept getting deeper and deeper into the forest.

The wolf, however, went straight to the grandmother's house and knocked on the door.

"Who is outside?"

"Little Red Riding Hood, bringing you cake and wine. Open the door."

"Just turn the knob," called the grandmother. "I am too weak and cannot get up."

The wolf turned the knob, and the door sprang open. Without

saying a word, he went over to the grandmother's bed and swallowed her. Then he slipped into her clothes, put on her cap, lay down in her bed, and drew the curtain.

Little Red Riding Hood had been running about in search of flowers, and when she had gathered as many as she could carry, she thought of her grandmother again, and she set out to her grandmother's house.

When she arrived, she was surprised that the door was open, and when she went inside, the place seemed so strange that she thought, "Oh, my goodness, how frightened I feel today, and usually I am so glad to visit Grandmother!"

She called, "Good morning," but received no answer. Then she went to the bed and pulled back the curtain. There lay her grandmother. She had pulled her cap way down on her face and looked so peculiar.

"Why, Grandmother, what big ears you have!"

"The better to hear you with."

"Why, Grandmother, what big eyes you have!"

"The better to see you with."

"Why, Grandmother, what big hands you have!"

"The better to grab you with."

"Oh, but Grandmother, what a dreadfully big mouth you have!"

"The better to eat you with."

No sooner had the wolf spoken those words than he jumped out of the bed and devoured poor Little Red Riding Hood.

When the wolf had sated his lust, he lay down in the bed again, fell asleep, and began to snore very loudly.

A hunter was walking past the house, and he thought, "How loudly the old woman is snoring! I ought to see whether there is anything wrong with her." He entered the house, and when he came to the bed, he saw the wolf lying there. "So there you are, you old sinner," he said. "I have been looking for you for a long time." He was about to aim his musket when it occurred to him that the wolf might have eaten the grandmother and that she might still be saved. So he did not shoot. Instead, he took a pair of scissors and began to cut open the belly of the sleeping wolf. After making a few slits, he saw the red riding hood. A few slits more, and the girl jumped out and cried, "Oh, how frightened I was, how dark it was inside the wolf's body!" And then the old grandmother also came out alive and could barely breathe. Little Red Riding Hood quickly got hold of some big stones. She stuffed them into the wolf's body, and when he awoke, he tried to leap away, but the stones were too heavy, and he sank down and dropped dead on the spot.

Now all three of them were overjoyed. The hunter stripped off the wolf's fur and went home with it. The grandmother ate the cake and drank the wine that Little Red Riding Hood had brought, and she recovered. But Little Red Riding Hood thought to herself, "I will never again leave the path by myself and run into the forest when Mother tells me not to."

The Boy Who Set Out to Learn Fear

A FATHER had two sons. The elder was very intelligent and knew how to adapt to everything. The younger, however, was stupid and could not understand or learn anything. And when people saw him, they said, "His father is going to have problems with this one!"

If there was anything to be done, then the elder son always had to do it. But if the father told him to fetch something in the evening or at night, and the road went past the churchyard or some other terrifying place, then the elder would answer, "Oh no, Father, I'm not going there, it's scary!" For he was afraid. Whenever stories were told by the fire in the evening, giving everyone goosebumps, those listening would sometimes say, "Oh, I'm scared!" The younger son would sit in a corner, listening, and he could not understand what was meant. "They always say, 'I'm scared! I'm scared!'" he thought to himself. "But *I'm* not scared. This must be a skill that I know nothing about."

Now, one day the father said to his younger son, "Listen, you, in the corner there, you're getting big and strong, you have to learn something so that you can earn your livelihood. Look how your brother makes an effort, while you're a hopeless case."

"Oh, Father," the son answered, "I would like to learn something. Yes, if it's possible, I would like to learn to be scared. I don't know anything about it."

Hearing this, the elder son laughed and thought to himself, "Goodness gracious, what a dummy my brother is. Nothing will ever become of him. Just as the twig is bent, the tree's inclined."

The father sighed and answered the younger son, "You'll learn how to be scared, all right, but you won't earn your livelihood with it."

A short time later, the sexton came for a visit, and the father told him his troubles, saying that his younger son was so inept at everything. He didn't know anything or learn anything. "Just imagine, when I asked him how he wanted to earn his livelihood, he actually wanted to learn how to be scared."

"If that's all he wants," the sexton replied, "I can teach him. Just put him in my charge and I'll lick him into shape."

The father liked the idea. He thought to himself, "He'll knock the corners off the boy."

So the sexton took the boy into his home and gave him the task of ringing the bell. After a few days, the sexton woke him at midnight, told him to get up, climb to the church tower, and ring the bell.

"You'll learn how to be scared, all right," the sexton said to himself, and he secretly went on ahead. The boy reached the top of the stairs, turned around, and was about to take hold of the bell rope when he saw a white shape on the stairs, opposite the louver window.

"Who's there?" the boy shouted. But the shape did not respond or move.

"Answer me," shouted the boy, "or get out of here. You have no business being here at night."

But the sexton remained motionless so that the boy would think he was a ghost.

The boy shouted once again, "What do you want here? Speak, if you're an honest fellow, or I'll throw you down the stairs."

The sexton thought to himself, "He doesn't really mean it."

He didn't make a sound, and he stood there as if he were made of stone.

The boy shouted at him a third time. And when he saw that this was useless, too, he charged into the ghost and knocked it down the stairs, so that it fell ten steps and remained lying in a corner. The boy then rang the bell, went home, got into bed without a word, and fell sound asleep.

The sexton's wife waited and waited for her husband, but he did not return. Finally, she grew frightened. She woke the boy up and asked, "Do you know where my husband is? He went up to the tower ahead of you."

"No," replied the boy, "but someone was standing on the stairs opposite the louver window. He wouldn't answer me and he wouldn't go away either, so I thought he was a thief and I pushed him down the stairs. Just go over and you can see whether it's him. I'm sorry."

The wife hurried off and found her husband. He was lying and moaning in a corner, and his leg was broken.

She carried him down the steps and then ran, screaming, to the boy's father. "Your boy," she shouted, "has done something terrible. He has thrown my husband down the stairs, and my husband's leg is broken. Get that good-for-nothing out of our home."

The father was frightened. He hurried over and gave the boy a sound scolding. "What kind of godless pranks are these? The Evil One must have inspired you."

"Father," answered the boy, "please listen. I'm completely innocent. He was standing there in the night, like someone who's about to do something bad. I didn't know who it was, and I warned him three times to either speak up or go away."

"Ah," said the father, "I get nothing but misery from you. Get out of my sight. I never want to see you again."

"Yes, Father, I'll be glad to go. Just wait until daylight, then I'll set out and learn how to be scared. That way I'll master a skill so that I can earn a living."

"Learn whatever you like," said the father, "it's all the same to me. Here are fifty gold pieces. Take them, go out into the wide world, and never tell anyone where you come from or who your father is, because I am ashamed of you."

"Yes, Father, whatever you say, if you don't ask for more than that. I can easily remember that."

At the break of day, the boy packed his fifty gold pieces into his pouch, went out to the great highway, and kept saying to himself, "If only I could be scared! If only I could be scared!"

Then a man came along, and he heard what the boy was saying to himself. When they had walked a bit, so that they could see the gallows, the man said to him, "Look, there's the tree where seven men have married the ropemaker's daughter, and now they're learning how to fly. Sit down underneath and wait until nightfall—then you'll learn to be scared."

"If that's all it takes," replied the boy, "that's easily done. And if I learn to be scared this fast, I'll give you my fifty gold pieces. Just come back to me tomorrow morning."

The boy then went to the gallows, sat down underneath, and waited until nightfall. Feeling very cold, he built a fire. But at midnight, the wind was so cold that the boy couldn't get warm. And when the wind blew the hanged men back and forth, making them knock against one another, the boy thought to himself, "I'm freezing down here by the fire—imagine how they must be freezing and shaking up there." And feeling pity, he placed the ladder against the gallows, climbed up, untied one man after another, and brought down all seven of them. Then he stoked the fire, blew on it, and sat them all around it so that they might warm up. However, they sat there without stirring, and their clothing caught fire. The boy then said, "Watch it, or else I'll hang you all back up again." But the dead did not hear; they held their tongues and let their rags burn away. The boy became angry and said, "If you don't watch out, then I can't help you— I don't want to burn up with you." And he hung them all up again, each in turn. Then he returned to his place by the fire and fell asleep.

The next morning, the man came to him, for he wanted to

get the fifty gold pieces. He said, "Well, do you know what it's like to be scared?"

"No," replied the boy, "how should I know? Those men up there never opened their mouths, and they were so stupid that they let the few old rags on their bodies burn."

The man saw that he could not get the fifty gold pieces. Going off, he said, "I've never met anyone like this before."

The boy, too, went his way and began talking to himself again: "Oh, if only I could be scared! Oh, if only I could be scared!"

These words were overheard by a drayman, who was walking behind him. The drayman asked, "Who are you?"

"I don't know," the boy replied.

"Where are you from?" the drayman went on.

"I don't know."

"Who is your father?"

"I'm not allowed to say."

"What do you keep mumbling to yourself?"

"Oh," answered the boy, "I wish I could be scared, but no one can teach it to me."

"Stop your chattering," said the drayman. "Come on, come with me. I'll find you a place to stay."

The boy went with the drayman, and in the evening they reached an inn, where they were to spend the night. When they entered the inn, the boy again said very loudly, "If only I could be scared! If only I could be scared!"

Upon hearing him, the innkeeper laughed and said, "If that's what you crave, then you'll have the opportunity here."

"Oh, keep quiet," said the innkeeper's wife. "A number of foolhardy men have already lost their lives. It would be a shame if those beautiful eyes never saw the light of day again."

But the boy said, "No matter how hard it is, I want to learn it. That's why I set out." And he gave the innkeeper no peace until the man told him that not far from the inn there was a bewitched castle where a man could learn how to be afraid if he just spent three nights there. The king had promised his daughter to any man who had the courage to try it. She was the most beautiful maiden under the sun. The castle also contained great treasures, guarded by evil spirits. These treasures would then be released, and they could make a poor man rich. Many men had already gone in, but none had ever come out again.

The next morning the boy went to the king and said, "If I may, I would like to spend three nights in the enchanted castle."

The king looked at him, and because he liked the boy, he said, "You may ask for three things to take with you into the castle, but they must be inanimate objects."

The boy answered, "I would like to take a fire, a lathe, and a carving bench with a knive."

The king let him carry all these things into the castle by day. When night was gathering, the boy went up into the castle, built a bright fire in a chamber, placed the carving bench and the knife next to the fire, and sat down on the lathe. "Ah, if only I could be scared!" he said. "But I won't learn it here either."

Around midnight he wanted to stoke up his fire. As he blew into it, a scream came from a corner: "Oh, meow, we're freezing!"

"You fools," he shouted, "what are you screaming for? If you're cold, sit down by the fire and warm up."

And no sooner had he said this than two huge black cats came over in giant leaps, settled on either side of him, and looked at him wildly with their fiery eyes. After a time, when they had warmed up, they said, "Comrade, why don't we play a round of cards?"

"Why not?" he replied. "But first show me your paws."

They stuck out their claws.

"Oh!" he said. "What long nails you have! Wait, I'll have to clip them first." Then he grabbed them by their necks, put them on the carving bench, and fastened their paws.

"Now that I've seen your fingers," he said, "I don't feel like playing cards." He killed them and threw them into the moat outside.

But when, having put the two of them to rest, he was about to sit down by his fire again, black cats and black dogs on white-hot chains emerged from every nook and cranny, more and more of them, so that he could not escape. Shrieking horribly, they stomped on the fire, pulling it apart and trying to put it out.

He watched them calmly for a while, but when it got too much for him, he grabbed his carving knife and shouted, "Get out of here, you riffraff!" And he slashed out at them. Some of them leaped away; the rest he killed and threw outside into the water. When he returned, he fanned the sparks and blew up the fire and warmed himself.

As he sat there, he grew drowsy and could no longer keep his eyes open. So he looked around, and he spied a large bed in the corner. "That's just right for me," he said and lay down in it. But as soon as he closed his eyes, the bed began moving by itself, and it moved through the entire castle. "That's right," he said, "faster." And the bed rolled away as if drawn by six horses; it rolled over thresholds and up and down stairs. All at once, *pow, pow,* it capsized, turned over, and lay on top of him like a mountain. But he hurled the covers and pillows into the air, climbed out, and said, "Let someone else do the traveling now." He lay down by his fire and slept until daybreak.

In the morning the king came, and when he saw the boy lying on the floor, he thought that the ghosts had killed him and that the boy was dead. The king said, "Too bad about this handsome man!"

The boy heard him, sat up, and said, "Things haven't gone that far!"

The king was astonished, but also delighted, and he asked the boy how everything had gone.

"Quite well," he replied. "One night's gone by, and the other two nights will also go by."

When he came to the innkeeper, the man gaped at him. "I never thought that I would see you alive again," he said. "So have you learned how to be scared?"

"No," said the boy, "it's all useless. If only someone could tell me how to do it."

The next night, he went back up to the old castle, sat down by the fire, and began his old litany: "If only I could be scared!"

When midnight came, he heard a noise and a banging, first

softly, then louder and louder. Then there was a brief silence, and finally a half-man came down the chimney, screaming loudly, and fell down in front of the boy.

"Hey," cried the boy, "half is missing. This is too little."

The noise began again, there was a raging and howling, and the other half also fell down.

"Wait," said the boy, "let me blow on the fire for you."

When he had done this and looked around again, the two pieces had joined together, and a horrible man was sitting in the boy's place.

"That wasn't part of the bargain," said the boy. "That seat is mine."

The man tried to push him away, but the boy wouldn't put up with it. He shoved him off violently and then sat down in his place again. But now more men came falling down, one after the other. They brought nine human bones and two skulls, and after setting up the bones, they played ninepins.

The boy also felt like playing, and he asked, "Listen, can I play, too?"

"Yes, if you've got money."

"Money enough," he replied, "but your bowling balls aren't round enough."

He took the skulls, inserted them into his lathe, and smoothed them out until they were round. "There, now you'll be able to play better," he said. "Hey! Now we'll have some fun!"

He played with them and lost a bit of his money. But when the clock struck twelve, everything and everyone vanished before his eyes. He lay down and calmly fell asleep.

The next morning, the king came and wanted to know what had happened. "How did things go this time?" he asked.

"I played ninepins," the boy answered, "and I lost a little money."

"Weren't you scared?"

"Oh no!" the boy said. "I had fun. If only I knew what it's like to be scared!"

On the third night, he saw down on his lathe again and said with great annoyance, "If only I were scared!"

When evening came, six huge men arrived, carrying a bier. The boy said: "Ha ha, that must be my little cousin, who died only a few days ago." He beckoned with his finger and cried, "Come over, cousin, come over!"

They placed the coffin on the floor, and he then went over to it and took off the lid. A dead man lay inside. The boy felt the dead man's face, and it was as cold as ice.

"Wait," the boy said. "I'll warm you up a little." He went over to the fire, warmed his hands, and placed them on the dead man's face, but the dead man remained cold. So the boy took him out of the coffin, sat down by the fire, placed the dead man in his lap, and rubbed his arms in order to get the blood circulating again. But none of this helped either, and then it occurred to the boy: "When two people lie in bed together, they keep each other warm." He brought the dead man to the bed, covered him up, and lay down next to him. After a while, the dead man grew warm and began to stir. The boy said, "You see, cousin, haven't I warmed you up!"

But the dead man cried, "Now I'm going to strangle you!"

"What!" said the boy. "Is this the thanks I get? Back into the coffin with you." He picked up the dead man, threw him into the coffin, and put the lid back on. Then the six men came and carried the coffin out again.

"I just can't get scared," said the boy. "I'll never learn how to do it here."

Then in came a man who was bigger than all the others, and he looked terrible. He was old and had a long white beard.

"Oh, you insect," he shouted, "you'll soon learn what it is to be scared, for you are going to die."

"Not so fast," answered the boy. "If I'm to die, then I'll have to have a say in the matter."

"I'll get you," said the monster.

"Easy now, easy, don't carry on like that. I'm just as strong as you and probably even stronger."

"We'll see," said the old man. "If you're stronger than I, then I'll let you go. Come on, let's try it."

The old man then led him through dark corridors to a blacksmith's fire. He took an ax and struck the anvil into the floor with one blow.

"I can do better than that," said the boy, and he went over to the other anvil. The old man stood next to him in order to watch, his white beard hanging down. The boy then grabbed the ax, split the anvil with one blow, and wedged the old man's beard into the crack.

"Now I've got you," said the boy. "Now you're the one who's going to die." Then he grabbed an iron stick and began smashing away at the old man, until the old man whimpered and begged him to stop. He said he would give him great riches.

The boy pulled out the ax and let him go. The old man led the boy back into the castle and showed him three chests of gold in a cellar.

"One chest is for the poor," said the old man, "the second is for the king, and the third is for you."

But now the clock struck twelve and the spirit vanished, so that the boy was left in the darkness.

"I'll make my way out," he said. Groping along, he found his way back into the chamber and fell asleep by his fire.

The next morning, the king came and said, "Now you must have learned what it's like to be scared."

"No," replied the boy. "Just what is it? My dead cousin was here, and a bearded man came. He showed me a lot of gold down in the cellar. But no one has told me what it's like to be scared."

The king said, "You have broken the spell on the castle, and you shall marry my daughter."

"That's fine," answered the boy, "but I still don't know what it's like to be scared."

The gold was carried up, and the wedding was celebrated. But as much as the young king loved his wife, and as much as he enjoyed himself, he kept saying all the time, "If only I were scared, if only I were scared."

In the end, this annoyed his wife. Her chambermaid said, "I'll do something about it. He'll learn to be scared, all right."

She went out to the brook that flowed through the garden, and she had the servants get her a whole pailful of gudgeons.

That night, when the young king was asleep, his wife pulled off his blanket and emptied the pail of cold water and gudgeons over him so that the little fish began to writhe and struggle all over him. The young king woke up and cried, "Oh, I'm so scared, I'm so scared, dear wife! Yes, now I know what it's like to be scared."

The Goose Girl

ONCE upon a time there was an old queen. Her husband had been dead for many years, and she had a beautiful daughter. As the girl grew up, she was promised to a king's son far away. The time came for the girl to marry, and when she was about to leave for the other kingdom, the old woman packed up a great many precious objects and jewels—gold and silver, goblets and gems—in short, everything that was part of a royal trousseau, for she loved her child with all her heart. She also gave her a chambermaid, who was to ride along with her and deliver the bride into the hands of the bridegroom. Each girl was given a horse for the journey. The princess's horse was named Falada, and he could speak.

When it was time to leave, the old mother went into her chamber, took a small knife, and cut her fingers, making them bleed. Then she held a white rag under her hand and let three drops of blood drip into it. Giving the rag to her daughter, she said, "Dear child, take good care of these drops of blood; you will need them along the way."

The mother and daughter tearfully took leave of each other. The princess put the rag into her bosom, mounted the horse, and rode off to her bridegroom.

After riding for an hour, she felt very thirsty, and she said to her chambermaid, "Dismount, take my goblet, which you have brought along, and fetch me water from the brook. I would so much like to drink something."

"If you're thirsty," said the chambermaid, "then get off your horse, lie down, and drink from the brook. I don't want to be your maid."

The king's daughter was so thirsty that she dismounted, leaned over the water in the brook, and drank, and she was not allowed to drink from the golden goblet. She said, "Oh, God!"

And the three drops of blood replied, "If your mother knew, her heart would burst in her body!"

However, the king's bride was humble, so she said nothing and mounted her horse again.

They rode a few leagues more, but the day was warm, the sun was penetrating, and soon she was thirsty again. When they came to a small river, she once again called to her chambermaid, "Dismount and bring me water in my golden goblet." For she had long since forgotten all the nasty words.

But the chambermaid said even more haughtily, "Serve yourself if you want to drink. I'm not your maid, whatever you think."

The king's daughter was so thirsty that she got off her horse, leaned over the flowing water, wept, and said, "Oh, God!"

And the drops of blood answered once again, "If your mother knew, her heart would burst in her body."

And as she drank, leaning over the water, the rag with the three drops of blood fell out of her bosom and floated away with the water, but she was so frightened that she did not notice it. However, the chambermaid had been watching, and she was delighted that she now had power over the bride. For once the princess had lost the three drops of blood, she was weak and powerless. When she was about to mount her horse Falada again, the chambermaid said, "I belong on Falada, and you belong on my nag."

And the princess had to put up with this. Then, with harsh words, the chambermaid ordered her to take off her royal garments and put on the chambermaid's poor clothes, and finally the princess had to swear an oath under the open sky that she would say nothing about any of this to anyone at the royal court.

And if she had not sworn this oath, she would have been killed on the spot. But Falada saw everything, and he remembered it.

The chambermaid now mounted Falada, and the true bride mounted the nag, and then on they rode, until at last they arrived at the royal castle.

There was great joy over their arrival, and the king's son came leaping toward them. He lifted the chambermaid off her horse, thinking that she was his bride. She was led up the steps, but the true princess had to remain below. The old king looked down from the window and observed her waiting in the court and saw how fine, delicate, and beautiful she was. He immediately went to the royal chambers and asked the bride about her maidservant who was standing in the courtyard, and he asked who she was.

"I took her along for company on the way here. Give the maid some work to do so that she doesn't stand around idly."

But the old king had no work for her and couldn't think of anything. So he said, "I have a little boy who tends the geese. She can help him." The boy's name was Kürdchen, and the true bride had to help him tend geese.

But soon the false bride said to the young king, "Dearest husband, please do me a favor."

He answered, "I'd be glad to."

"Call the flayer and tell him to cut off the head of the horse that I rode here, because it annoyed me during the trip."

Actually, however, she was afraid that the horse would speak and tell them what she had done to the king's daughter. But now her wish would come true, and loyal Falada would die. The news reached the true princess. And she secretly promised the flayer a bit of money, which she would pay if he performed a small service for her. The town had a big, dark gate, through which she had to pass every evening and every morning with the geese. She told the flayer to nail Falada's head there, so that she could see it frequently. The flayer promised to do so. He cut off the head and nailed it to the dark gate.

Early every morning, when she and Kürdchen passed through the gate, she said as she went through:

Oh, you, Falada, hanging there.

And the head replied:

> *Oh, you maiden queen when you went,*
> *If your mother knew,*
> *Then her heart would be rent.*

She quietly went out of the town, and they drove the geese into the field. And when she arrived in the meadow, she sat down and loosened her hair. Her hair was pure gold, and Kürdchen saw it and was delighted by its shine, and he wanted to pull out a few of her hairs. But she said:

> *Woe, woe, little wind,*
> *Take Kürdchen's little hat*
> *And make him chase it*
> *Until I've braided up my hair*
> *And put it up again.*

And a wind came, and it was so strong that it blew Kürdchen's hat across the countryside, and he had to run after it. By the time he came back, she had finished combing and braiding her hair, and he could not get any hairs. This made him angry, and he would not talk to her. And so they tended the geese until evening, and then they went home.

The next morning, when they went out under the dark gate, the maiden said:

> *Oh, you, Falada, hanging there.*

Falada replied:

> *Oh, you maiden queen when you went,*
> *If your mother knew,*
> *Then her heart would be rent.*

Outside the town, she sat down in the meadow again and began to comb out her hair, and Kürdchen ran over and tried to grab it, but she quickly said:

> *Woe, woe, little wind,*
> *Take Kürdchen's little hat*
> *And make him chase it*
> *Until I've braided up my hair*
> *And put it up again.*

The wind blew, and it blew his cap off his head, and it blew it so far that he had to chase after it. And by the time he came back, she had long since finished with her hair, and he could not seize a single strand. And so they tended the geese until evening.

That evening, however, after they had come home, Kürdchen went to the old king and said, "I do not want to tend geese with that girl anymore."

"Why not?" asked the old king.

"Oh, she bothers me all day long."

The old king then commanded Kürdchen to tell him about her. Kürdchen said, "In the morning, when we pass through the dark gate with the flock, there is a horse's head on the wall, and she talks to it. She says:

> *'Oh, you, Falada, hanging there.'*

"And the head answers:

> *'Oh, you maiden queen when you went,*
> *If your mother knew,*
> *Then her heart would be rent.'*

And then Kürdchen told the old king about what had happened in the goose meadow and how he had been forced to run after his hat in the wind.

The old king ordered him to drive the geese out again the next day. And as soon as it was morning, the old king sat down behind the dark gate and listened to the girl talking to Falada's head. And then he followed her into the meadow and hid behind a bush. Soon, with his own eyes, he saw the goose girl and the goose boy driving the flock. After a while, she sat down and unbraided her hair, and it was bright and shiny. Then she said again:

> Woe, woe, little wind,
> Take Kürdchen's little hat
> And make him chase it
> Until I've braided up my hair
> And put it up again.

A puff of wind came and carried off Kürdchen's hat, so that he had to run a long way, and the maid quietly combed and braided her hair, and the old king observed everything. Then he returned, unnoticed, and when the goosegirl came home in the evening, he called her aside and asked her why she did all those things.

"I cannot tell you. I cannot lament my fate to any human being, for I have sworn an oath under the open sky. Otherwise I would have lost my life."

He urged and urged her and left her no peace, but he could not get anything out of her.

Then he said, "If you do not want to say anything to me, then lament your fate to the iron stove." And he went away.

She crept into the iron stove, began to moan and weep, and, pouring out her heart, she said, "Here I sit, abandoned by all the world, and yet I am a king's daughter, and a false chambermaid has forced me to take off my royal garments, and she has taken my place with my bridegroom, and I must do common chores as a goosegirl. If my mother knew, her heart would burst in her body."

The old king was standing outside by the stove pipe, eavesdropping. He came in again and told her to get out of the stove. Her royal garments were put on her, and her beauty was a miracle to behold. The old king called his son and revealed to him that he had the wrong bride—that one was merely a chambermaid, while the true bride was standing here as the former goosegirl. The young king was overjoyed when he saw the princess's beauty and virtue, and a great feast was ordered, to which all people and good friends were invited. At the head of the table sat the bridegroom, the king's daughter on one side and the chambermaid on the other. However, the chambermaid was dazzled, and she did not recognize the king's daughter in her radiant adornments.

When they had eaten and drunk and were merry, the old king asked the chambermaid a riddle. What was a woman worth if she had deceived her master in such and such a way? And he told her the whole story and asked, "What judgment does she deserve?"

The false bride said, "She deserves nothing better than to be stripped naked and put in a barrel lined with sharp nails; and two white horses should be harnessed to the barrel, and they will drag her to her death, from street to street."

"That woman is you," said the old king, "and you have named your own judgment, and it shall be carried out on you."

And when the sentence was carried out, the young king married his real wife, and they ruled their kingdom in peace and happiness.

FAIRY TALES AND CHILDREN

A Private Foreword

~~~~~~

*W*HO *really understands children?* In 1947, when I was a young
teacher, I got to teach a class of my own for the first time. There
I stood, in front of thirty second-graders, a horde of dirty, hungry, lice-ridden kids. They all lived in Quonset huts in a German
refugee camp, and the school stood right in the middle of the
camp, a shack made of thin wood and black corrugated iron,
just like the huts the children lived in.

I had volunteered for this school, for these were the children
I wanted to help. I plunged into my new task with complete
enthusiasm. The children needed a great deal of attention, this
was clear to me, and I was ready to give them my best.

We had been taught that the love and affection we give children is gratefully requited. This was an error. On the third day,
they filched my wallet from my briefcase, and at the end of the
first week, a boy named Heiner poured ink into the new aquar-
ium so that all the fish died. Still, I remained friendly. But my
pupils were noisy, quarrelsome, and unwilling to learn anything.
The classroom was truly silent only when the kids were allowed
to paint. We did a lot of painting. Otherwise, I wouldn't have
made it through the first few weeks.

Then came my birthday, and everything changed abruptly.
The pupils, whom I had begun to think of as little devils, brought

35

candles to school and left presents on my desk. These presents were real treasures in the second year of the postwar era: a herring, cigarettes, soap, a bag of potatoes. The children quietly got to their feet and respectfully sang "Happy Birthday!" I was deeply moved.

The next day, everything was forgotten, and the class was as unruly as ever. I was completely at sea about these children. I had once thought I understood them. After all, one does know children, doesn't one? And I had assumed I could deal successfully with a class of eight-year-olds. But now all these puzzling things were happening.

I was confused, perplexed, and pretty much at the end of my rope. I needed help, and so I visited my uncle. He was a psychiatrist, a professor by now, and had always been a friendly authority on all problems of life for me and other members of the family.

"Do you understand children?" I asked him. "Do you know what children are all about?"

He leaned back comfortably in his large chair. "Tell me what's on your mind," he said.

I told him everything. And I was so agitated that by the time I finished, my face was red. "Well," I asked him again, "what are children all about?" I was young and impatient.

He gently shook his head. "I don't know," he said. "Who knows children?"

I glared at him in disappointment.

"In any case, they're different," he said, standing up and walking over to the bookcase. He took a brown volume from the top shelf, glanced at the book for an instant, then gingerly blew the dust off the cover, smiled, came back, and handed me the book.

I did not smile. The book was Grimms' *Fairy Tales*. He was undaunted by my horrified expression.

"This book," he said, "contains everything that anyone can know about children." And then he amiably went on: "But you probably don't know how to glean that knowledge from these stories." He walked back to the bookcase and pulled out various tomes. Freud, Jung, Adler, a good half-dozen. "These will help you," he said.

They did help me. However, it took me half a lifetime to gain even a little understanding of fairy tales. I still cannot claim that I understand children, but I do know a little more about them now, if only because of my study of fairy tales.

Of course, fairy tales were no remedy for my discipline problems in school. But nevertheless, they did help me.

Every Saturday I told my class a fairy tale, and this was the loveliest hour of the week for them. The children were even quieter than when they painted.

Do fairy tales know children? Do these simple tales really understand more about children than an experienced psychiatrist who has raised two boys and a girl?

No question about it. My uncle was right. Once you've learned to read between the lines and detect the subliminal truths beneath the surface plot, you are amazed at what lies concealed in the fairy-tale characters.

And the most fascinating of these characters are the children: Hansel and Gretel, Snow White, Strong Hans and Hans-in-Luck, Tom Thumb and Rose Red. These children are anything but well-behaved reflections of parents' wishful thinking. They are really different, and they have typically childlike lives of their own. They love, suffer, and hate. They steal and lie. They are kind-hearted and self-sacrificing. They are selfish and jealous. They pursue their goals rigorously, and they always triumph in the end, whereupon they let their enemies die deliciously horrible deaths. Yes, that's what children are like more or less.

And needless to say, they also do all the things that people don't talk about. Indeed, children are not the only ones. Fairy tales are stories about wishes, and these wishes come true. The sky's the limit. Fairy tales flout not only the laws of nature, but most other laws as well, including good manners, ethics, and the Ten Commandments. Only the facade is sweet, dear, and pure— sometimes. Behind it, nature dominates, and a rather primal life is always seething there. Using vivid and at times drastic images, fairy tales depict the things that touch human beings and drive them, the things they hope for and long for. On the surface, these are suspenseful stories. But underneath, they contain ancient and traditional wisdom, experience and knowledge concentrated by the centuries. These tales were passed on by word of mouth. They were shaped by generations of storytellers. The best stories survived; these are the ones we still know today.

Fairy tales are popular poetry, for they originated and developed among the people. They were born in fusty spinning rooms. Simple people told them to simple people. No one else was interested in these "old wives' tales." No superior authority, whether profane or ecclesiastic, exerted any influence. Fairy tales developed outside the great world, beyond the centers of political and cultural power. They absorbed nothing from these areas, no historical events, no political facts, no cultural trends. They remained free of the moral views, behavioral standards, and manners of the various epochs.

The many kings and queens in fairy tales have no historical background as in the sagas. Their lofty titles may indicate that they have power and sway, that they rule. But they never rule a kingdom. Their only subjects are children. The kings and queens are parents, the princes and princesses their children. Nor is any royal castle here real, nor did it ever exist. The castles are homes, and the kingdoms are families.

Fairy tales are not interested in pomp and circumstance or in status, rank, or title; they are interested in human beings. Simple people with their worries, problems, and conflicts are the heroes of these stories. Human beings per se are the focal point of fairy tales, and people are pretty much alike no matter when or where they have lived.

Children at the North Cape and in the Far East have very similar problems with themselves, with their parents and siblings, and with the opposite sex. This is why so many identical and similar fairy-tale themes can be found in different countries even in other cultures throughout the world.

Independent of time and space, fairy tales depict basic patterns of life and experience, universal situations, typical behavior of children and parents, fundamental data of human relations.

It was exciting and interesting to follow these plots critically, to trace the lives of their heroes, and to ask what their actions meant. The results were often astounding, even unexpected insights into the essence and behavior of boys and girls, and there were several surprising answers to the question what children are really all about.

Fairy tales also revealed how intricately the lives of children are interwoven with the lives of other people and how significant their relationships to their parents and siblings are. It became clear how important and decisive for their futures the relationships of boys and girls to their mothers and fathers are. Here, fairy tales touch upon problems of upbringing. Naturally, fairy tales do not solve these problems, but they very plainly show the premises for solutions. Free of any era's theories, ideologies, and dogmas, these stories offer glimpses into the vital needs of parents and children and into relationships within families. They take us back to the place where every upbringing begins, to fundamentals that we have often lost sight of in today's flood of information.

Throughout history, there have been very disparate opinions on children and how to raise them. But never before have there been so many different views on children and on their treatment and upbringing as in our present society. There are almost no universal norms or standards left in the way people raise children today. Anybody can advocate anything and apply any method of education. And this is exactly what happens, both in public and in private. The educational style varies from school to school— even from class to class—and from family to family. Indeed, the differences are often extraordinary. Some parents are extremely conservative. They demand strict obedience, orderliness, cleanliness, and industriousness; they want a well-behaved, conformist child. Other parents are just as one-sided in their progressiveness. They advocate new ideas and ideals, rejecting anything that smacks of the past, and they want a free and emancipated child.

In between lies a gamut of nuances. The great mass of parents are unsure of themselves. Many have resigned.

The following reflections of fairy tales will, I hope, shed some light on this dismal scene. May some of the happy-go-lucky attitude of fairy-tale heroes rub off on us and reconcile us with children, and may it liven up the day-to-day path of education. I also hope that certain insights about that "unknown being," the child, will elicit a smile or two from parents, a chuckle, perhaps even deeper thoughts about and clearer insights into their own and their children's situation.

In any case, I wish all readers a lot of fun and a little profit when reading this book.

CARL-HEINZ MALLET

Notes on Methodology

IN this book, fairy tales are treated as a source of insight into the nature of children and parents. However, I am not focusing on fairy tales in the usual way. Instead, I infer from them a meaning and a purpose that cannot be read all that easily into their plots. This approach may seem strange to some readers, but it is not arbitrary; I use methods developed by depth psychology and verified by fifty years of dream interpretation, becoming a recognized practice.

Many researchers have applied the technique of dream interpretation to literary material. Carl Gustav Jung was one of the most important of these scholars. And a number of scholars have thus discovered concealed and previously undetected meanings in folk and fairy tales. The first to do so was Sigmund Freud in 1913 (fairy-tale subjects in dreams in *Collected Papers*, Vol. IV).

Other authors have also interpreted fairy tales. But in surveying the countless publications, we cannot say that scholars of various directions have come to the same conclusions. On the contrary: fairy-tale interpretations by different authors often have little in common.

Understandably, some critics feel that one can read anything into both dreams and fairy tales, with no limits on speculation. However, if we study the material more closely, we find that

41

dreams, and especially fairy tales, are extremely complex and thus have many layers of meaning. Like life itself, they offer a wealth of aspects, and no one can grasp all of them. They thus leave room for very different approaches.

Nevertheless, we do have a sufficiently reliable criterion for assessing and evaluating the various interpretation attempts: subjective opinion. In the interpretation of dreams, it is the dreamer who decides whether an interpretation is correct. He will accept only what sounds plausible to him, no matter how solid the theoretical foundation of the analysis may be. The same applies in our area. It is the reader who has the final word. He will follow and accept the interpretations only so long as they convince him or at least sound cogent.

He must, however, bring along a bit of goodwill. For the things lurking behind the familiar tales of the Brothers Grimm are frequently unusual, extraordinary, and sometimes even dreadfully astounding. Often, they are of a sexual nature.

I would like to take three German folk songs and use them as examples to show what lies ahead for the reader and what method I will use in examining and interpreting fairy tales.

If folk songs are transmitted orally and are not art songs whose authors are known, then their history is similar to that of fairy tales. They developed among the people and were handed down from generation to generation. The following song comes from the Memelland, the region north of the Memel River.

Zogen einst fünf wilde Schwäne,
Schwäne leuchtend weiss und schön.
Sing, sing, was geschah?
Keiner ward mehr gesehen, ja.

Wuchsen einst fünf junge Birken,
grün und frisch am Bachesrand.
Sing, sing, was geschah?
Keine in Blüten stand.

Once, five wild swans went off in flight,
Swans so lovely and radiant white.
Sing, sing, what happened then?
None was ever seen again.

Once, five young birches grew,
Green and fresh by the edge of a brook.
Sing, sing, what happened then?
None of them ever bore a bloom.

On the surface, the song tells of animals and trees that have no connection and yield no plot, no story. Still, there *is* an emotional impression: swans that never return and birches that never blossom arouse melancholy. Scientifically, of course, one can argue that birches, at least normal ones, do not bloom and thus cannot bear flowers. For the critical reader, this may be the first hint that the real subjects are not birches and perhaps not swans, that the depicted scene shows only one side, namely the surface and not the real side, and that there is a second side, the real and essential one.

Our example proves, for once unequivocally, that this is indeed the case. This song is actually about people. The text itself reveals the second side, the other aspect, and, if one employs the vocabulary of depth psychology, the latent meaning behind the manifest content.

The song goes on:

Zogen einst fünf junge Burschen
stolz und kühn zum Kampf hinaus.
Sing, sing, was geschah?
Keiner kehrt' nach Haus.

Wuchsen einst fünf junge Mädchen
schlank und schön am Memelstrand.
Sing, sing, was geschah?
Keins den Brautkranz wand.

Once, five young boys went off to fight,
Proud and bold, off to war.
Sing, sing, what happened then?
None of them came home again.

Once, five young maidens grew,
Slim and fair by the Memel's edge.
Sing, sing, what happened then?
None of them wove a bridal wreath.

The real subject here is, as so often, human problems: departure, separation, abandonment; men who die and girls whose sweethearts are taken by war and who do not achieve the goal of their lives—young birches who will never bear flowers.

They symbolic imagery illustrates the events, helps to express the mood, and appeals to the emotions.

In all our discussions, we will be dealing with the two sides presented above. Of course, from now on, only one side will be available to us. The second side will have to be grasped with the aid of depth psychology, imagination, and critical thinking.

In the next song, too—it comes from Silesia—the two related levels are quite easy to recognize.

Es blies ein Jäger wohl in sein Horn,
und alles, was er blies, das war verlorn.
Soll denn mein Blasen verloren sein?
Viel lieber möchte ich kein Jäger sein.
Er warf sein Netz wohl übern Strauch,
da sprang ein schwarzbraun Mädel heraus.
Ach, schwarzbraunes Mädel, entspring mir nicht,
Ich habe grosse Hunde, die holen dich.
Deine grossen Hunde, die fürchte ich nicht,
sie kennen meine hohen, weiten Sprünge nicht.
Deine hohen, weiten Sprünge, die kennen sie wohl,
sie wissen, dass du heute noch sterben sollst.

Ja, sterbe ich heute, so bin ich tot,
begraben mich die Leute ums Morgenrot.
Er warf ihr das Netz wohl über den Leib,
da ward sie des jungfrischen Jägers Weib.

A hunter blew into his horn,
And everything he blew was lost.
Must everything I blow be lost?
I'd rather not be a hunter then.
He cast his net across a bush,
A dark brown maiden then sprang forth.
Oh, dark brown maiden, don't run away,
I've got big dogs, they'll chase you down.
Your great big dogs, I fear them not,
They do not know my high, far leaps.
Your high, far leaps, they know them well,
They know you have to die today.
Ah, if I die today, then I'll be dead,
The people will bury me at dawn.
He cast his net across her body,
And she became the young, lively hunter's wife.

Like so many others, this hunting song is not about a hunt for hares, stags, or does; it tells about catching a far nobler prey. Nor is this concealed here.

The hunter's initial blowing is no death halloo at the end of a hunt. It is a young man's wistful mating call, which, like that of many men who are too young, at first has no responsive echo. The hunter realizes that blowing his horn is not enough, he has to do more than that. When he does do more—that is, casts his net over the bush—the girl he longs for appears in the flesh. But she does not just sink into his arms, she runs off. He timidly says, "Oh, dark-brown maiden, don't run away." But his plea is no more effectual than his threat to set his dogs on her. Nevertheless, a dialogue ensues; the girl reacts, and the hunter instantly becomes more sure of himself and tells her that she'll have to die today.

Here, to be sure, normal logic is of no help in following the story any further. However, generations of Germans have sung the song in this way and never been bothered by what happens. Was their sense of the latent meaning, the essence of the story, more powerful than their logical thought, their ratiocinative processes?

Even less comprehensible is the rest of the song. The girl says, "Ah, if I die today, then I'll be dead, / The people will bury me at dawn." What, we must ask, do death and burial have to do with the encounter between a young man and woman?

Here, we are helped by the experiences of the psychology of dreams. It is by no means unusual for a dream to present an idea in terms of its exact opposite; burials frequently indicate weddings, coffins a bridal bed. Such a reading offers itself here, too, and it fits into the description: the girl would like to have a wedding. And in regard to death, this image is not as farfetched as it may initially appear; for when a girl marries, she loses a number of things, which she has to "bury": her freedom, her name, and, last but not least, her innocence.

Conceivably, the hunter may not construe "death" in the same way. We will have to live with the ambiguity of notions and symbols; dreams and fairy tales are not mathematical equations to be solved with formulas, and there is no way to gain an understanding of human beings with mathematics. At any rate, the young hunter's first thoughts are not of a wedding or of "people." He has released his big dogs, which represent the sphere of his drives. They want to pursue the girl, to chase her down. The hunter is after her "body"; he throws his net over it, and she becomes his wife under the net. This is his version, these are his wishes. He would like to consummate the marriage "naturally." For him, her "dying" means "becoming his prey." The song thus depicts the male viewpoint.

The girl, to be sure, does not put up much of a fight and makes no more use than necessary of her "high, far leaps." In any case, she lets him catch her, and she dreams of the wedding. This is her version, the female viewpoint. The cheerful, optimistic mood of the song leaves no doubt that her wish comes true.

This text speaks freely of sentimentalities, reservations, and misgivings; but it is equally free of morals in telling its love story. It reflects life and love in a fresh, natural, light-hearted way, and this is certainly one reason for the long survival of this folk song, which is still sung throughout Germany.

An altogether different mood emanates from the East Prussian song "Es dunkelt schon auf der Heide" (The heath is darkening now). It lacks the merriment and optimism of the hunting song. A sad story takes place against the background of a day in late summer: a girl is deserted; the "natural marriage" is not followed by a real wedding.

> *Es dunkelt schon auf der Heide,*
> *nach Hause lasst uns gehn!*
> *Wir haben das Korn geschnitten*
> *mit unserem blanken Schwert.*
>
> *Ich hörte die Sichel rauschen,*
> *sie rauschte durch das Korn,*
> *ich hörte mein Feinslieb klagen,*
> *sie hätt ihr Lieb verloren.*
>
> *Hast du dein Lieb verloren,*
> *so hab ich doch das mein,*
> *so wollen wir beid miteinander*
> *uns winden ein Kränzelein.*
>
> *Ein Kränzelein von Rosen,*
> *ein Sträusselein von Klee.*
> *Zu Frankfurt auf der Brücke,*
> *da liegt ein tiefer Schnee.*

Der Schnee, der ist geschmolzen,
das Wasser läuft dahin.
Kommst du mir aus den Augen,
kommst mir nicht aus dem Sinn.

In meines Vaters Garten,
da stehn zwei Bäumelein.
Das eine, das trägt Muskaten,
das andre Braunnägelein.

Muskaten, die sind süsse,
Braunnägelein sind schön.
Wir beide, wir müssen uns scheiden,
ja, scheiden, das tut weh.

The heath is darkening now,
Let us go home!
We've cut the rye
With our naked sword.

I heard the sickle soughing,
It soughed through the rye,
I heard my sweetheart lamenting
That she had lost her love.

If you have lost your love,
I still have mine.
So let us go together
And weave a little wreath.

A little wreath of roses,
A little bouquet of clover.
A deep snow is lying.
In Frankfurt, on the bridge.

The snow, it has melted
The water flows away.
You may be out of my sight,
But not out of my mind.

In my father's garden,
Two saplings now stand.
One tree, it bears nutmeg,
The other, cloves.

Nutmeg is sweet,
Cloves are beautiful.
We two, we have to part,
Ah, parting is such pain.

This song, too, does not hide the fact that it is telling a love story; but the symbolism is of an altogether different sort.

No net is used as an image here. A net is meant to catch, hold fast, take possession. The "naked sword" is quite another matter.

First of all, no one uses a sword to cut rye. This indicates quite plainly that the song is not about cutting rye or havesting, but that this image is a metaphor. The sword that hangs at the man's side, his ornament and weapon, of which he is proud and with which he wants to fight his way to many victories, is here—as very often in dreams—a sexual symbol. However, it is far more than just male sexuality. It points to a certain widespread male attitude toward sexuality and the opposite sex. It involves vanity and aggressiveness: The sword thrusts in.

The man in this song has little similarity to the young hunter. This time, there is no mating call, no dialogue, no wooing, but merely the sickle soughing through the rye. He is the sickle, she the rye. There is no commitment, no exchange, no relationship. Sword and sickle cut and separate, and the rye falls. This is not a romantic process, but a mechanical and loveless one. The girl does not even appear; she has no profile, no features. She is only quoted and called "sweetheart," which merely romanticizes a not very decent way of quickly turning a girl into a forgotten beloved.

He remains unmoved, but she laments that she has "lost her love." This is true, and she will never regain it: never regain love—for he does not return it—or her innocence. She thus loses something that he cannot lose, and he is tactless enough to reproach her for it.

The hope for a wedding, so obvious in the song about the hunter, is frustrated here. A "little wreath" is also round, but it is a far cry from being a wedding wreath, and the nosegay he offers her is merely worthless clover. He begins his retreat and does not mince his words: "A deep snow is lying / In Frankfurt, on the bridge." Snow is cold, as cold as his feelings about her now. His mind is already elsewhere, in Frankfurt, his hometown. This is where his father's house is, and in the garden, two "saplings" wait for him, with noble blossoms, sweet and beautiful. They have little in common with a farmgirl. He does tell her, "You may be out of my sight / But not out of my mind." But even a guileless reader will take this as shoddy comfort.

The song is over, and so is the brief affair. "We two, we have to part, / Ah, parting is such pain." Painful for her, no doubt, but certainly not for him.

As these examples show, the texts cannot be read schematically, they cannot be "translated." Nor does it suffice merely to insert familiar symbols. The technique of depth psychology can only be an aid, which, if used without imagination and empathy, may easily lead to all too simple and gross interpretations—for instance, if one sees the "naked sword" only as a penis.

Needless to say, these interpretations are speculative, and this holds for all such efforts. As a rule, however, they rely not just on one piece of evidence, but on several, which frequently confirm one another. Furthermore, every reading must fit into the context, and the story emerging from the hidden (repressed) contents must be consistent with the mood expressed by the manifest text, and it must be cogent. These conditions expose any number of misinterpretations.

Hansel and Gretel

The story of two children with highly exacting wishes, which place their lives in great jeopardy, a situation dealt with by the prudence and energy of the girl.

THE poor woodcutter lives outside a great forest with his wife and his two children, Hansel and Gretel. They are so badly off that they do not have enough to eat. The man, too worried to sleep, tosses and turns in his bed, sighs, and asks his wife, "What's to become of us? How can we feed our poor children if we don't even have enough for ourselves?"

One of the best-known fairy tales of the Brothers Grimm begins with this description of an oppressively hopeless situation. It begins not with the children, but with the parents, and this makes sense, for the parents are the decisive factors in this story: they initiate the action.

This is true not only in this fairy tale. It is a fundamental truth: parents are their children's destiny. That is why the woodcutter and his wife must be given their due attention.

The way the fairy tale depicts the man and woman will make anyone take sides with them immediately. Any reader, young or old, will spontaneously sympathize with the worries of the harassed father. And we will indignantly reject the behavior of the mother, who coldly and soberly suggests that they abandon their children in the woods. "They will not find the way home again, and we will be rid of them," she says.

Naturally, the man protests; he does not want to do it. He cannot bring himself to leave his children alone in the forest, abandoning them to the wild beasts. "No, wife," he says, "I will not do it." She calls him a fool and points out that now all four of them are going to starve to death and that he might as well plane the boards for their coffins. She gives him no peace until he finally agrees. "I feel so sorry for the poor children," he says.

No one will understand how a mother can behave so heartlessly. The Brothers Grimm themselves had their misgivings, for they altered the original text of the story. They made such changes frequently, as they pointed out in their preface. They own up to improving style and diction, "omitting any expression not suitable for children." But they added nothing, they say, and never altered the essence of the story. For, as they explain in their preface, their chief goals were fidelity and truth.

However, they were not all that faithful or true in this story. They changed a highly essential feature. In their edition of the original version, the fairy tale unequivocally speaks of a *mother*. The Grimms changed this word to "wife" seven times; twice, they changed the parents or the father and mother into "the old ones"; and finally, they turned the mother into a (wicked) step-mother. And that settled the matter: As far as anyone else is concerned, Hansel and Gretel now have a stepmother.

In this case, the Brothers Grimm are responsible for the step-mother. Now, the enormous number of stepmothers in fairy tales can certainly not be blamed on the Grimms; but all those stepmothers must have been created by a similar mechanism. Since mothers cannot be cruel, wicked, cold-hearted, and unloving, they became stepmothers; for after all, one could not defame an entire class of people, certainly not the noble category of mothers.

Many tellers of fairy tales must also have turned mothers into stepmothers. They transferred the problem to a (defenseless) minority, thus hurting no one, not the mothers, and not the children, who might have easily been made to feel insecure with so many wicked mothers.

The victims of this objectively unfair transfer were and are the real (mostly very loving) stepmothers.

I have my doubts, however, that storytellers made Hansel and Gretel's mother into a stepmother. Probably not. For nothing tangible points in this direction. Fairy tales usually do not hold back with clear and unequivocal judgments; they call the good good and the bad bad. But this fairy tale is different. Not a single sentence characterizes the father as positive or the mother as negative. If we place value judgments on the parents, labeling the father good and the mother bad, then this is nothing but our spontaneous reaction, which, in this case, however, suggests itself quite plainly—but only because we identify with the heroes of the tale, the children. To them, the mother must obviously seem wicked. Nor is this true only here; it is a normal tendency among children. For them, every mother becomes a wicked mother if she opposes their wishes, makes demands, or restricts their freedom. Children do not ask themselves whether a mother is correct in doing so. They hate even necessary parental guidance. This attitude of children is another reason why there are wicked stepmothers in fairy tales. They are wicked only from the viewpoint of their egotistical offspring, who love their comfort and do not want to take orders.

Hansel and Gretel's mother is even planning something especially evil. She wants to send the children into the forest, desert them, forsake them, leave them to starve, abandon them to the wild animals. No wonder this mother becomes a wicked stepmother. After all, she is truly and obviously wicked, beyond any doubt.

Yet she's not. She only seems to be. The situation appears altogether different when we put ourselves in the parents' shoes. They do not have much latitude in their situation. They really have only two alternatives: either all four starve to death or two survive. If the entire family is not to perish, then only the second possibility can be chosen. And if one asks who should survive, then there is only *one* realistic answer: the parents. The children would not be able to make it on their own.

In these circumstances, the mother appears in quite a different light; for those are her very thought processes. She is not wicked or evil. She sees the desperate situation in objective terms, and she thinks about it. This is the best one can do under the circumstances. Her suggestion is not hard-hearted; it is the only logical conclusion to be drawn from the given facts. She undeniably finds a way out of the hopeless situation.

To some, this justification will sound solid and correct; but it will nevertheless cause a certain uneasiness and will not make the woodcutter's wife any more likable. This is understandable, for she does not correspond to our notions of a likable woman. She is not passive, she does not submit, she is anything but "the little woman." And she corresponds even less to the usual image of a mother, from whom one demands love, nurturance and sacrifice. She evinces none of these traits. There is absolutely nothing soft, emotional, or sentimental about her. On the contrary, her arguments are intelligent, logical, and to the point. What she says is cogent, and her husband has to give in.

He, likewise, in no way corresponds to the usual notions of a husband and father. He is neither strong nor superior, neither logical nor objective, and he is a far cry from being what is known as the "master of the house." He worries, tosses and turns in bed, and racks his brains. But nothing comes of his effort. He only asks, "What is to become of us?" He does not know the answer. He does not suggest any solution. "He did not know how to help himself in his plight," goes the original version. He merely sighs and pities his poor children. He neither hits on an idea nor acts. He is merely sentimental, and, if we think about it, this is one thing he cannot afford to be, for his sentimentality endangers the life of the entire family. Might he truly be the fool that his wife calls him? In any case, the traditional roles are reversed. He merely sighs and moans, while she thinks and acts. If we look at the plain facts, the scene states that the man is weak and emotional, and the woman strong, logical, and reasonable.

Psychologists have always maintained that this is true, and all modern investigation has confirmed it. The astonishing thing is that this insight can be found in an ancient fairy tale. Equally remarkable is the fact that such conduct is taken for granted here and depicted with an utter lack of polemics. The husband is not mocked and the wife is not called domineering. Neither is maligned. In just a few lines, a terse and extraordinarily concentrated description makes the parents come alive and reveals an essential and correct insight into male and female roles.

Psychologists have known for a long time that men have a harder time surveying, judging, and resolving emotional problems than women do. Men tend to react with their feelings; normally, they are as helpless in such situations as the woodcutter in the fairy tale and, like him, they are dependent on the active energy of their wives.

Many men do not care to identify with this behavior. They are often ashamed of it.

Hansel and Gretel's father is not the least bit ashamed. He is true to himself and to his sentimentality. He has no doubts and does not try to conceal his soft core behind a rough exterior. He shows his feelings and his uncertainty. He wages no power struggle with his wife, does not even argue with her, nor does he feel wounded in his "male ego." He states his opinion, but does not try to get his way by means of violence. On the contrary, he gives in. (Later, it will turn out that he was right to do so.)

The woodcutter shows what many men are really like. It is not fair to find him disagreeably unmanly. At least, children do not see him in this way, and this is good. The fairy tale presents a very human and natural father. He has nothing in common with the man who still functions as a model in our society and in whose image a considerable number of our sons are still being reared. No sooner can they walk than they are taught that boys do not cry or play with dolls and that, in any event, they are better than little girls.

The most unusual feature of this fairy tale is the depiction of the mother. It does not overlap with the image of a mother who, by virtue of her maternal love, must be prepared to make any sacrifice and who is free of any selfishness, any thought of herself.

Such a mother image is sentimental, unrealistic, and just as exaggerated as the false image of the man.

This fairy tale pulls both figures off their unsuitable pedestals and brings them down to earth. The father is no hero and the mother is neither a demigoddess nor a "dear little mother." She is practical, and in no way cruel or hard-hearted. Nor is she selfish, and she does not wish to kill her children. Something entirely different is going on behind the surface plot. If we read the text carefully and critically, we realize that the family's problem is not their physical plight. It is not bread that they lack. The four are not on the verge of starvation, nor are they bitterly poor.

They live, we are told, outside a huge forest with a great deal of wood. They have a house of their own, not a shanty. It has a white chimney, a large door—a Dutch door—and presumably a workshop. In any case, the father has boards and a plane. The path to the house is strewn with shiny pebbles. Hansel wears a "little coat" and owns a white kitten and a dove. Gretel has an apron. All these things appear friendly and cozy, but not poor. The family certainly does not lack its daily bread. Something else is missing. Hunger is only a symbol. It shows that there is something that does not suffice for all of them, and this lack endangers the family.

I would like to submit that the deficiency is not material and that bread stands for love, affection, and tenderness. People do not have an infinite supply of these things. When too much is asked of them, they have to husband their resources. This is the problem confronting the woodcutter's family, and it is obviously the children who take so much that the parents have nothing left for themselves. That is why, says the mother, the children have to go into the forest. She wants to light a fire for them, and each child is to receive a piece of bread.

At this point, one must ask whether such a problem can be so serious as to justify the image of great want, of looming starvation. Can the difficulty of "budgeting" love and affection imperil a family as profoundly as the fairy tale would have it? And does this situation have parallels in the ordinary reality of present-day family life and education? I believe that such parallels exist.

The starvation depicted in this fairy tale is something that many married couples experience with their children. It begins with the banal fact that the parents can no longer be alone and undisturbed—certainly not in the daytime, and at night they can never be sure that they will not be bothered.

This purely external problem is shown in the fairy tale when Hansel and Gretel eavesdrop on their parents' very private conversation.

Oddly enough, however, most married couples do not seem at all aware of this problem; they never think about it, much less discuss it with one another. Hence, they never make plans for dealing with the new situation. And by no means do they talk about the effects that the new situation will have on their mental and personal sphere. This is why most parents do not even realize what is happening. They fail to perceive what and how much their children deprive them of. Nor do they ever notice how their marital relationship is altered. This regrettable development goes through well-known phases, which anyone can observe in numerous marriages.

The beginning of any two-way relationship is mutual fondness. Love and affection are in the foreground and are perceived as beautiful and blissful. For many, it is the high point of life; and this is their first mistake.

The term "high point" characterizes the situation: after that, it's all downhill. The time of this love is brief, nothing but a point in our existence. The reality of colloquial speech does not even measure this time in months. Just one month: the honeymoon. This is all the more amazing when we recall the high priority of love in our society. How often people have sung and written about "eternal love" and "living happily ever after."

The oft-cited "happiness of love" ends very frequently with the birth of the first child. All at once, everything is over, everything that the young couple felt to be the most important thing in the world for them and that they believed would last a lifetime. Many people view this development as something like a law of nature, an inalterable phenomenon. But this is not true. Most couples do not lose their love—they give it up voluntarily, if unwittingly. They do it for the children. For their sake, they sacrifice their personal relationship, and most parents do not even realize it. Normally, it happens the moment they stop using a first name or endearment with each other. Instead, they address each other as Dad and Mom or Daddy and Mommy. And this is often the point at which their love life flattens and peters out. It becomes empty, unstimulating, routine, a conjugal duty (what an expression!). It stops being an experience, it no longer satisfies, it no longer provides the couple with energy. The couple relationship loses more and more meaning. The previously normal affection and attentiveness keep diminishing and often vanish altogether. What used to be given to the spouse is now given to the children. The children are the new focal point of life, and the husband and wife are now nothing but parents. They no longer talk about themselves, about their own wishes and needs. They talk about the children and the weekly grocery list. Love, actually no infinite potential, is frittered away in daily family living. The husband and wife grow dissatisfied, and the children are not happy either in this dreary situation.

Some marriages collapse under the strain. Others turn bleak, becoming marriages of habit or quarreling. Common to them all is the end of the love between husband and wife, and this lack deprives the family of its foundation.

In contrast, there are couples who stick it out, who do not grow apart or become indifferent to one another or destroy themselves by quarreling. They then frequently experience a second high point of their love, a late "honeymoon," which often lasts longer than the first and is more enduring. These couples find one another anew, when their children grow up and leave home. This once again makes it clear that children cause the starvation. They can do so because the parents do not think about it; they are unaware of the danger.

And that is the distressing part: one cannot blame children for their parents' marital problems. This will not do, it is taboo. Children are the "salt of the marriage"; they can never be anything else. They have an unwritten right to be the center of the family. They come first, and everything else is secondary. Parents who think of themselves first and of their children second are considered cruel.

The woodcutter's wife thinks of herself and her husband first. She wants to survive with him, and she talks about it. She does exactly what so many couples fail to do. Her actions are sensible, and she is right. She realizes that the couple, the mutual love of the parents, constitutes the basic relationship in the family and must be preserved. This relationship is primary; being a mother or father is secondary. For the woodcutter's wife, the parents come first and the children second. This is the prerequisite for a happy family life.

And what does she get for her attitude? The status of a cruel mother. She is instantly stripped of the honorable title "Mother"; now she is merely a wife and eventually a wicked stepmother. She undergoes something that so many people endure when they advocate something unusual, though correct: She is terribly maligned.

This is obvious when one reads the text carefully. The story is structured in such a way that every reader is bound to assume that the wicked stepmother is deliberately planning the certain death of her children. But this is not true. She does not say a word about it. She wants to send the children into the forest with a piece of bread for each of them. In terms of our reading, bread signifies love and affection. She also wants to light a fire for them; and in Ludwig Bechstein's version of the tale, she commends the children to the good Lord. None of these things sound like murder plans.

It is the father who speaks of the children's certain death. He assumes that the wild animals will tear Hansel and Gretel to bits. But he is seeing ghosts. The later part of the story shows that there are no wild beasts in the forest, only "thousands of little birds." One of these birds is white and sings very beautifully. That is all. No animal tears the children to bits.

However, Hansel and Gretel do not know this in advance. They eavesdrop on their parents, and what they overhear must make them fear the worst. They learn that their lives are at stake, and they have no reason to doubt it. Gretel tells her brother, "We're doomed." Even if one excludes the possibility of physical death, for the children do not die, the situation nevertheless remains cruel enough. The two children are threatened with desertion, abandonment, separation from their parents, solitude, the loss of the entire foundation of their mental and physical existence.

At some point in their young lives, children learn for the first time that they can be left alone, that the mother's constant presence is not to be taken for granted. If they are unprepared for this realization, then it can trigger the worst anxieties and inflict a lasting shock on their sense of life. Many never recover from this experience, and the fear persists. It is a primal fear of children, of all human beings, for not even adults can stand being alone and isolated.

The fairy tale depicts a situation that, if it were real, would be one of the worst that a child could go through. A child who was actually faced with such a situation would plunge into deepest despair or wildest panic.

But not Hansel and Gretel. The boy is not the least bit upset by what they have heard; he remains utterly calm and unimpressed. Gretel, at least, sheds a few tears, but shows no further concern. Both children remain lying in bed, as cool as cucumbers, until their parents fall asleep. Truly a respectable achievement.

I believe that the reaction of the two title characters is one reason why this fairy tale is so popular among younger children. The latter will have to wrestle with their fear; they are still dependent on their mothers and cannot get along without them.

They cannot be thrown back on their own resources. The sheer thought of being deserted triggers an existential angst in the truest sense of the word, and justifiably so. However, this problem is far less pressing for older children. Nor are they interested in Hansel and Gretel; they have other fish to fry.

Now when I picture what goes on in children who hear or read this fairy tale, I can understand the Brothers Grimm, who claimed their stories had a "benedictory power." Such an expression may no longer be our cup of tea today. But I would certainly say that this passage of the tale has a highly beneficial effect. For it can put a fearful child at ease, especially one who fears that when his mother leaves, she will never come back. Since scarcely any child is free of fear, all children can find solace in Hansel and Gretel, who have no fear and keep their heads up high even in the worst possible situation, who seek a solution and find it, who—and this is very important—use their own devices to free themselves and return wealthy. This vicarious experience is lots of fun for a little boy or a little girl; it makes them feel free and relieved, it strengthens and promotes their development. In scenes like this, in my opinion, fairy tales have an extraordinarily powerful pedagogical effect.

To be sure, only Hansel shows this splendid composure. Gretel remains lying in bed, quite resigned, and sadly gives in to her fate. Not Hansel. He acts. He gets up and steals through the dark house. This alone will make him a hero for many children. After all, most of them are scared of the dark. But Hansel is not afraid. He opens the bottom of the Dutch door and leaves the protective house. The night does not faze him any more than his solitude. The bright moon shines on the white pebbles in front of the house, making them glow like silver coins. Hansel bends down and stuffs into his pocket as many pebbles as it can hold. Then he returns to Gretel, comforts her, tells her she can fall asleep without fear, and he gets into his own bed.

He is really quite a boy. Bold, active, and dauntless, he gains control of the situation. He shrewdly hits on a plan, and he is friendly and helpful to boot. He almost perfectly fits the ideal conception of a "real boy." His sister, in contrast, offers an altogether different image. The girl is passive, unimaginative, perhaps even stupid. All she does is weep.

Unlike their parents, the two children seem to fulfill the traditional male and female roles. But, as so often in fairy tales, this is a mere facade; which can be proved right here.

It is clear what Hansel is planning. He intends to use the pebbles to mark the way so that he can find the route back home. This is a smart idea, no doubt, and it shows that he has a good head on his shoulders. But if he *is* intelligent, then he ought to realize that their return will change nothing. His clever trick is unproductive; it does not solve the family problem. The family will not gain a single crumb of bread. His plan helps no one, not even him.

Hansel is by no means as smart as he at first appears. He would have to starve, just like his sister and their parents. His action is as worthless as the stones he gathers. They only shine like silver coins, but they are not silver. Hansel does not deserve a reward.

The decisive deed will subsequently be carried out by Gretel. It is she who pushes the wicked witch into the oven, thereby freeing her brother and bringing about a happy, generally beneficial ending for the story and for all concerned. Then comes the deserved reward; not worthless pebbles, but chests of gold and jewelry.

Hansel and Gretel do not embody the usual male and female roles. No child will find a confirmation here that boys are active and intelligent, forming a superior caste, while girls are only second-class citizens.

However, they are often treated in this way, and this is shown not just in fairy tales. It is one of the rules of protocol in real, genuine, present-day European royal dynasties that when a female child is born to the ruling couple, the guns fire only half the salute that they fire when a prince is born. It is certainly not due to the monarchic example that commoners have similar misgivings; many fathers (and mothers?) are more joyful about a "son and heir" than about a "mere" girl.

Fairy tales do not make this value distinction. In the Grimm collection, just as many of the title heroes are girls as boys, and both villains and heroes are sometimes male and sometimes female.

The next morning, Hansel and Gretel are awakened roughly. "Get up, you lazybones," says "the wife," giving them the promised bread. "This is all you are getting," she adds. At least, that's what we read in the Brothers Grimm. However, the original version sounds a wee bit different: "The mother . . . awoke the two of them: 'Get up, children, we are going to the forest. Here is a piece of bread for each of you. But be careful with it and save it for lunch.' "

One can understand the Grimms. After turning the mother into a wicked stepmother right at the start, they could not let her wake the children in a friendly way. "The wife" had to remain wicked. The Grimms were stuck with her.

So off the family goes, Hansel bringing up the rear. He keeps lagging behind, stopping, looking toward the house, and, we read, doing this "over and over again." His actions draw attention, and the father eventually asks him, "Hansel, why do you keep looking back? Pay attention and keep walking!" The boy is caught in his secret activity, and anyone unfamiliar with the story will wonder how Hansel deals with the situation. This is what happens. "Oh, Father," he says, "I am looking at my white kitten sitting up on the roof. It wants to say goodbye to me." He tells a lie, and the fairy tale makes no bones about it. It expressly says that he is not looking at the white kitten, but throwing a pebble on the road. Yet hardly a reader or listener will conclude: "How awful! The boy's lying!"

Such a reaction would be generally unusual, for one does not criticize the fairy-tale hero with whom one identifies. One assumes that he is good and will do no wrong.

But in this special situation, no one—whether identifying with

Hansel or not—will expect the boy to tell the truth. He quite obviously cannot afford to do so. It is, of course, regrettable that children lie; but every child does so sooner or later. Most parents know it. Very few parents believe that only other children lie, but not their own.

Yet this example shows that there are times when children have the subjective right to lie. They lie because they have no choice. It is impossible for them to tell the truth, and we parents ought to respect this, just as we not only forgive Hansel for lying, but even approve of what he does. Of course, we will very seldom encounter such a situation in real life. For when children lie in this way, we will not be able to tell that they are lying.

Hansel shows how to do it. First of all, he is not frightened, he does not hesitate, he is not even unsure of himself, and he reveals no hint of a bad conscience. Nor does he have one. Why should he? He maintains his composure. "Oh, Father," he begins, and anyone can imagine the artlessness with which Hansel gazes up at his father.

Hansel, as a fairy-tale hero, is not exceptional; he is typical. This is exactly how our children lie as they stare right into our faces with their big, honest eyes. We could swear on a stack of Bibles that they are telling us the truth; and we would be sadly mistaken.

Since, for the above-mentioned reasons, we have little hope of catching our sons and daughters in the act of lying, we should, without blushing, recall our own childhood lies. Such self-scrutiny can yield highly interesting glimpses into children's abilities in this area.

The content of Hansel's false statement is also interesting. He tells a poignant story—and not by chance. He is quite calculating in his use of an excellent tactic. For if his father believes him, then he has to assume that his son is naive and guileless, and he will never think him capable of doing what the boy is actually doing at this very moment. The father will simply never realize that Hansel is following a clear plan to thwart his parents' intentions.

The boy does it. His plan works. And many plans of our own children work equally well. We are skillfully fooled, tricked, and manipulated by them far more often than we realize. Their "tactical conduct" is not, of course, carefully thought out, meticulously planned. It is instinctive, unreflected, with few ifs, ands, or buts. Furthermore, they act swiftly. They intuitively grasp a situation or the person they are dealing with, especially his weak points. They react quickly and with astonishing sureness. They possess faculties that we lost long ago, and they employ them every day. Normally, we fail to notice.

However, most of us will remember how quickly we caught on to the weaknesses of our teachers and knew how to deal with these people, how far we could go and when to stop. Children have this ability not just in school. They do the same with us parents; often, even better, for they know us very well. Quite early in their lives, they master the usually successful method of pretending to be small, innocent, and guileless. This method works, for we treasure this image of a child; it fits in with our wishful thinking. Naturally, such wishes lead to false appraisals of reality, especially to an often enormous misjudgment of the actual level of knowledge and development that our sons and daughters have attained. Most of them do not believe in Santa Claus or the stork to the extent that their parents think they do. And there are many other things that we fail to credit our children with.

Hansel's father believes his son. The mother is more realistic, but she falls for his story. Of course, she does correct him. "Fool," she says, "that is not your kitten, that is the morning sun shining on the chimney."

She calls him a fool. She regards him as naive and stupid, and, just like the father, she fails to guess Hansel's real intentions. Hansel and Gretel know a lot more. They know what their parents are up to.

This fairy tale resembles a frequent reality: children are better oriented about their parents' plans, goals, and opinions than vice versa. This is quite natural, for they keep a very sharp eye on us. This is how they learn. They watch us day after day, taking in what they observe and, at some point, adding it to their own behavioral repertoire. Our conduct molds their conduct far more effectively than any instruction. It is therefore quite conceivable that Hansel and Gretel will someday deal with their own children the way their parents are dealing with them now.

At this point, however, such an idea would be unthinkable for them. They hate nothing so much as what their parents are up to, and they try to prevent it with any trick at their disposal. They resist and they refuse. They have only one goal: to return. They look neither to the right nor to the left. The huge forest, the beauties of nature, do not attract them. They do not even glance at them. All Hansel does is halt and peer back. He is characterized by his stopping, looking back, and moving back. He drops the pebbles so that he and his sister can return. The children want to go home again. But what have they done there so far? They've lain in bed and gone hungry. Nothing else. It is only when they find out that they could lose their warm beds that Hansel, at least, gets into gear. His knowledge induces him to act.

However, his activity is not progress; it serves no positive development. He does not wish to experience anything new. He is neither enterprising nor adventurous. Quite the contrary: he has done and is doing anything he can to maintain the status quo. This was the only reason he roused himself to act, the only reason he gathered the pebbles. The mother is right to interfere and take the children to the forest. There, they are bound to have the experiences necessary for their age. And the father, too, keeps driving Hansel, who always lags behind. "Pay attention and keep walking," he says.

When they reach the middle of the woods, the children can no longer act spontaneously. The father orders them to gather twigs. Then they become lethargic. They don't even play.

The father builds the fire for them, but this does not inspire them either. Yet almost any child is fascinated by fire. Nor is it pure chance that fire enthralls; like almost nothing else, fire is a milestone in the development of mankind. Human civilization began with the harnessing of fire. It plays an overwhelming part in mythology: Prometheus stole it from the gods.

But this magic medium leaves Hansel and Gretel cold; it does not interest them. The crackle of the burning twigs and flickering flames mean nothing to the children. They only feel the warmth. It is a surrogate for their lost beds, and it makes them feel tired. So "they slumbered a bit," says the Bechstein version. By noon, the fire goes out. They eat their bread. But they are still so tired that their eyes shut again. They fall fast asleep, sleep all afternoon and evening, and do not wake up until the middle of the night. Gretel cries.

The two children do not act their age. Sleeping all day, waking up at night, and crying—this is a baby's rhythm. Sleep, food, and warmth are their only interests, and that's all. Hansel and Gretel wish to remain infants. This is where their vital interests lie and have lain from the very start.

Their desire is not as objectionable as it may seem at first glance; for that kind of life-style can be quite pleasant. You are cared for, looked after, fed, and kept warm. You can sleep a lot, and you don't have to do a thing. The two children cling tight to this kind of life. They will not give it up without a struggle. They do not want their umbilical cord to be cut a second time. They have their experiences here, and these experiences are absolutely negative. From their perspective, growing up is nothing else than giving up one privilege after another.

They are right. Nothing is harder than growing up, and this is true from the very first, terrible day of our lives. From the soft, well-tempered security in the womb, we are born, amid the worst pain, into a world of coldness, discomfort, and discord. We have every reason to bawl our hearts out.

At least, a mother is there to comfort you, give you food, love, and affection. But before long, you feel your solitude, a terrible sense of abandonment. You scream, but no one comes. You experience something awful: your mother is not part of your personality. You have to come to terms with this realization.

Finally, you're not fed anymore; you have to eat on your own. More and more things are expected of the little human being, and the parents get angry if he doesn't do everything they demand.

We parents usually notice the progress that our children make, and we rightfully delight in it. But the opposite is true just as often. Children keep resisting. They don't want to get big. They push the spoon away because the bottle is more comfortable. They make in their pants again. They don't want to sleep alone. And so on and so on. We are familiar with all these things. Children are conservative, and they have a good number of reasons to be conservative.

Hansel and Gretel symbolize this childlike tendency. They don't care about the forest, the wide world (into which other fairy-tale heroes go so gladly), or adventures suitable to their age. They want to go back to their mother's apron strings, and no effort is too great for them. They walk all night long; the pebbles point the way. At daybreak, they arrive at their home.

The father is overjoyed. The mother's reaction differs in the various versions of the fairy tale. In Bechstein, she does not know whether to scold them or be happy. So she is glad, too, even though she would rather the children had remained in the forest.

There is one point in which the interests of parents and children coincide: We love our children, just as they love us. We, too, enjoy our closeness to them and are happy that they belong to us entirely and need us. If we train them to become independent, we do so more out of a sense of parental duty than because we really want them to become independent. We, too, have a private, selfish interest in keeping them small and dependent, for we know that they move further and further away from us with every step in their development, until they eventually leave us altogether.

Thus, there is children's selfishness and parents' selfishness. And there is voluntary renunciation out of love. Such renouncing is done by mothers who do not attach their children to themselves unnecessarily, who do everything to let their children become free and independent, who make their own needs secondary to those of their children.

The woodcutter's wife is such a mother. She realizes that the time has come for her children to spread their wings and that it is her duty to toss them out of the family nest. The two of them are no longer so little, they no longer have to be fed without doing something for themselves. They are no longer babies, and they finally have to leave their warm beds. They've outgrown their beds and are mature enough to camp out in the woods and make it on their own.

If children are not given such opportunities, are not considered capable of doing their own thing, are spoiled and kept little, they quickly develop into such pests that we regret bringing them up so badly. They become so exasperatingly selfish, so endlessly demanding, that the parents really have nothing left for themselves.

Hence, it comes as no surprise that soon after the children return, everything is consumed again. The mother wants to take Hansel and Gretel back to the woods, this time farther in, and the door is locked, so Hansel cannot gather pebbles.

The husband, we are told, has a hard time going through with it, and he feels it would be better if the mother shared the last bit of food with the children.

He feels what many people feel. The notion of obligatory maternal sacrifice is widespread. Such a mother is almost a primal image in our society, giving the word "mother" a sort of halo and thus overloading it. This image is thrust upon a young woman when she has her first baby. She is now a mother, something different, something new. She often stops being a woman. She chokes on her motherhood, sees nothing but her children, and forgets her husband.

The mother in this fairy tale has no such halo. She does not wish to sacrifice herself; she does not fit the primal image. That is why she was no mother for the Grimms, but "only" a woman. At least, that is what they turned her into. She does not make the sacrifice that her husband expects of her. She knows it would be wrong and senseless; she does not listen to him, she even reproaches him, pointing out that if you're in for a penny, you're in for a pound. He realizes she is right. He has gone along with her once; the situation has not changed—so he cannot say no this time. The action continues; the recess comes to an end.

The children eavesdrop again. Hansel tries his old trick, the pebbles, but it no longer works. The door is locked. However, he comforts his sister, saying the good Lord will help.

The next morning, Hansel improvises and strews bread crumbs along the way.

This device is very different from the first one. The pebbles seemed and proved to be a perfect device for what he was planning. But bread crumbs are pretty much the last thing in the world that one would use for such a purpose. So many other possibilities would be conceivable; yet Hansel uses, of all things, bread. He ought to know that birds will eat it; nevertheless, he uses it.

He is no longer the active, intelligent boy that he was the first time. Now he does not stop to think, nor does any idea come to him. He does not rely on his own resources; he places his trust in God. Hansel is slipping, he has gotten worse, and will not succeed this time. The adventure of returning has not strengthened his powers, has not brought him further. On the contrary. But why bread, of all things? Bread is the central problem of the family. It is the most valuable thing they possess, for they are starving. Once again, nearly everything has been consumed. They literally have only a morsel left. The children are so hungry they can't fall asleep. But what does Hansel do with the precious gift? He haplessly throws it on the ground. This boy cannot really be hungry.

Bread, we have said, is love. Children need love as badly as their daily bread. This is no claptrap, no facile truism. It is a proven fact. Children die without love, literally. Not even a baby monkey can survive if no mother is there to give it love.

The mother gives Hansel a piece of the last half-loaf of bread that the family has. He does not appreciate it. He wastes this valuable gift, does not want it.

Thoughtlessly, he throws it away; he cannot really have given it a second thought.

For Hansel, love is not vital; he does not suffer any lack of it. He has received more than enough. He is so sated that he crumbles the precious bread and throws it away.

Hansel rejects love. Anyone who knows children is familiar with this process. Such conduct is one of the most effective devices that children employ with adults. There is a whole scale of possibilities here. Everyone knows the sulky child who obstinately and nastily repels the hand that lovingly reaches out to him in reconciliation. Or the punished child whom you feel sorry for, whom you want to make friends with again, but who says no and feels a secret triumph. Or the child who, after an argument that you thought was settled, resumes hostilities in bed that evening and turns his face away with pursed lips, rejecting the goodnight kiss.

Depending on their temperament and the situation, children reject affection, flaunting their lack of interest when we try to do something nice for them, or unfeelingly denigrating a gift that we have brought them. One of their subtler methods is to rebuff friendly praise or brusquely retreat when we agree with them.

Sometimes we adults try to bring up a child by doling out love and tenderness. Often we fail to notice that our children employ this same tactic just as effectively as we, and usually even more effectively. Let's be honest: doesn't it jolt us when they reject our friendly and loving overtures? And doesn't their rejection always make us feel pretty foolish?

Children sense these reactions and exploit them even more effectively the next time. Some parents thus even become totally dependent on their children, and the plight of these mothers and fathers is truly distressing.

In Hansel's case, this is no ordinary situation of rejecting love. His problem is a fundamental one. He has received enough affection. Now he has to convert what his parents have invested. He ought to develop strength, energy, self-sufficiency, industry, and initiative; and in order to do so, he must finally leave his infantile, passive attitude. He has to learn how to get along with less affection. Yet this is the very thing he refuses to do.

What his mother gives him is the suitable travel provender for a new phase in his life. But Hansel does not want this ration. He does not want to leave, he does not want to travel, he does not want to go into the forest. He wants to return home. He forgoes the bird in his hand, preferring the two in the bush. Indeed, he wants a great deal more. In any case, he rejects his mother's development aid. What does he do with it? He crumbles the bread in his pocket, then he drops the crumbs. This is an abuse both in regard to bread and in regard to love.

Gretel is ahead of him in this respect. She has not "misused" her bread. She shares her piece with her brother, and they eat it. This is the correct approach in every way. Bread is meant to be eaten, and love is something to be shared. Hansel does not do this. He lags behind alone and crumbles the bread in his pocket. This is an entirely egocentric action, and his preoccupation with himself is not surprising in this situation. His mother no longer wants him, and he is not attracted by the adventures planned for him in the forest. Hansel therefore stagnates, occupying himself, almost by way of solace, with himself.

Everyone now expects the unpleasant word "masturbation." So far, I have deliberately avoided it, for Hansel is still small. What he does is qualitatively quite different from the masturbation of older boys, of adolescents. In puberty, bodily processes are involved, a physical urge is worked off, sexual notions and fantasies are decisive factors. All these things are absent from smaller children. They may do the same thing, but it is altogether different. It is really absurd to use the same term for it.

The parents do not notice what Hansel does, and this is the simplest solution. Normally, we never discover our children masturbating. And the way things are in this area, this has its advantages. In any case, we are spared having to be startled or dismayed by such an early "sexual activity" and having to resort to nonsensical or even harmful "pedagogical" measures.

This is really a tricky area, if for no other reason than because the famous Professor Sigmund Freud had an impact that was ill-fated in this case. He conjectured, quite correctly, that children are capable of feeling sensual pleasure at a very early age, initially when they suck the mother's breast. He found that they had oral, anal, and genital forms of satisfaction, which he called the "sexuality of children." He should not have used this expression.

Needless to say, one cannot object to his insights; they are correct and were confirmed by later researchers. However, I regard his term as inaccurate. It has fostered grave misunderstandings, to the detriment of parents and children. The reason is obvious. Sexuality is something quite unequivocal for us. It describes an essential aspect of our adulthood. It is a word for physical love and its fulfillment, for passion and desire, for the drives pulling us toward the opposite sex.

What we regard and experience as sexuality has just about nothing to do with what little children do and feel. It is something altogether different; it has an absolutely different quality. It is one of the crucial characteristics of children that they do not have our sexuality, do not know it or feel it, and, consequently, cannot understand it.

This difference is very clearly shown by the fairy tale in the different attitudes toward the bread. For the parents, its meaning is cardinal. They—and only they—suffer a lack and are hungry. They know and appreciate the value of bread. The children do not.

By no means am I saying that children are neuters when it comes to love. Quite the contrary. They have their own world in this area, with a similar, albeit quite different wealth of feelings, desires, and wishes. Normally, we adults know little of this world.

But when children occasionally play with their genitals, this usually has nothing whatsoever to do with that world and has as little in common with sex as sucking a thumb.

What is misnamed "sexuality" among them, because of a misunderstanding of a scientific definition, is nothing but the banal discovery by little children that several places on their bodies can generate nice feelings if properly touched. Mostly, they make these discoveries by chance when exploring their bodies. As a rule, they soon lose interest. But in critical situations, children sometimes resume these practices. As Hansel does.

He needs this comfort because he has withdrawn from his parents. However, he does not rebuff their love ostentatiously and defiantly; such conduct would annoy and provoke his mother, which is not his intention. The occurrence lies deeper. He takes the piece of bread. It would never cross his mother's mind that he would not eat it. He fools her and conceals his feelings. He breaks off the attachment, not temporarily, because of a passing whim, but for good. He considers his mother wicked and evil. She has disappointed him, refusing to give him what he wishes and imagines; she even wants to get rid of him and fobs him off with a piece of bread. He does not care for this. He goes by the motto "If I can't get everything, then I don't want anything."

Since there is no other person to whom he can turn here, he makes do with himself. He can comfort himself only very briefly in his flight from reality. Reality quickly catches up with him. When the moon finally rises, he takes Gretel by the hand in order to return home as they did the first time. But the bread crumbs are gone, devoured by the "thousands of little birds" in the forest.

If you were to believe that Hansel and Gretel are terribly frightened and despairing now, you would be mistaken. Children frequently do not react as we expect and assume. Often, they are tougher and more robust than we think, especially when their vital (usually egoistic) interests are at stake. At such times, they do not give up so easily and are not so readily intimidated.

Thus, Hansel and Gretel are anything but dismayed; they neither moan nor weep, they do not lose heart, they are not adversely affected.

This is not because they are particularly courageous or intelligent. They only imagine they are. Actually, they think too highly of themselves, view themselves as the center of the world—because they have been the center of the family far too long. They think they can do anything; they believe they know everything and are capable of everything. "I'll find the way home," says Hansel, and pulls Gretel along.

He doesn't find the way home. They walk all night and all the next day, from dawn to dusk. By now they are so tired that they fall asleep. This time, I grant, they deserve their rest. They are, understandably, hungry, too, and they feed on "nothing but a few berries" from the wayside. They are accustomed to more and better food; yet they are far from starving. The Brothers Grimm say that if help does not come soon, they are "certain to perish." But I regard this as an exaggeration. This is, I feel, only the children's impression of the situation. They not only over-estimate themselves, they also make big demands. Such an attitude is not unfamiliar. There are enough children who want to make us think that they will be seriously harmed if we do not make their wishes come true. They demonstrate this for us with all the mimic, verbal, and theatrical devices at their disposal. They argue, complain, weep, and act absolutely miserable. Admittedly, these scenes are often convincing. Nevertheless, they do not "perish" if we fail to give in. Nor do Hansel and Gretel perish.

Still, these often quite irritating show-offs have their strong sides. No wonder, for the love and care that children receive give them strength and power and the basic self-confidence so important in making one's way in life. But when "giving" is overdone, the parents run the risk of being exploited by the children, because the latter use their "strength and power" to keep the parental wellsprings flowing and getting as much as possible out of them. This is the opening situation of the fairy tale.

Hansel and Gretel, extremely well provided with everything to the point of impoverishing their parents, are physically and mentally fit and in top form. They could hike for a long time, and they have no trouble dealing with the realization that they are not getting out of the woods. Nevertheless, little has changed in their rhythm. Their life still alternates between eating and sleeping; the only addition is the great amount of walking. But they still do not perceive their surroundings. They do not hunt for berries, but eat only those that happen to be growing along the way, and they sleep under any tree. They take only what the forest offers them with no effort on their part.

Their basic needs are filled by the woods. But the children do not give this a second thought. They still refuse to develop; they remain babies, insisting that others act for them and take care of them. They still fail to understand that they must finally do something themselves. They never even dream that they could build a shelter or look for food systematically. Nor do they climb up a high tree in order to reconnoiter the terrain. They do keep walking, but aimlessly and shiftlessly. They make no sensible effort to find their way out of the forest. They are and remain "consumers," focusing purely on consumption and taking it for granted that the parents produce, and produce for them.

Some fantastic adventure would be suitable for the two of them, and the forest would offer the right conditions. But they do not accept the offer. The shock of being abandoned has not sparked their development. On the third day, a bird sings in a tree. There is nothing special about this, for we have learned that there are thousands of birds in the woods, and presumably they have not held their beaks. But this time, the children stop in their tracks. And another astonishing thing happens: they listen to the bird. This is indeed a remarkable achievement for these two egocentrics. For the first time, they break through their self-centeredness and focus on something else. And then something promptly happens: the bird, "a lovely snow-white bird," flies ahead of them, and they follow it.

However, this animal does not strike me as all that real. It does not in any way resemble a real forest bird. It is not like any titmouse or woodpecker, and the doves in the forest are not white. One can scarcely expect realities now.

The bird flies to a house, and when the children get very close to the house, they see that the "cottage" is made of bread, the roof is covered with cake, and the windows consist of "white sugar." Here it is, world-renowned, the witch's gingerbread cottage, life-sized, livable, bigger than any that the modern cake industry has ever managed to construct. This house has conquered the hearts of all children. A real dream house.

Indeed, such a house can only be dreamt. Hansel and Gretel dream it up. Again, they refuse to perceive reality. They flee into this grandiose dream.

Moderation is not the forte of spoiled children. And this image shows how immoderate they can get.

If you follow the educational rule of making children's wishes come true, then you know what lies in store for you. If you do not brake and steer the demands of children, then their primal dream takes this shape: they want not pounds of goodies, but a whole house made of them. Anyone consistent enough to fulfill this wish, too, can be quite certain that the children would ask for more, once the house was built. Children are limitless in their demands. And the fulfillment of immense wishes does not make them happy. Quite the contrary.

Hansel and Gretel waste no time. "Let's start in and have a fine feast," says Hansel, deciding to tackle the sweet roof. He tells his sister, "Eat the window, Gretel, that's nice and sweet for you."

Truly, the boy is undaunted. His frustrations of the last few days allow no doubts to emerge in him. He still considers himself the superior party, in command, and generously tells his sister what she should eat. He is so conceited that he believes he has a better idea of what's good for Gretel than she does herself.

This, too, is a well-known trait of children. They easily lose a sense of their real dimensions. They order their brothers and sisters around, and, if permitted, they consider themselves more intelligent than their fathers and mothers.

Some even try to deal with their parents in those terms, frequently when one parent is alone. Boys living with their mothers love to assume the father's role. They are as "solicitous" as Hansel is with his sister, feel responsible for their "Mommy," tell her what she has to do, comfort her when she has worries, and imagine that they know what's good for her. They play the "man of the house," often with no sense of humor whatsoever.

Our hero and heroine dig in. Hansel breaks off a piece of the roof, and Gretel nibbles on the panes. Suddenly, from inside, come the now famous words:

> *Nibble, munch, and crunch!*
> *Who's eating my house for lunch?*

One must bear in mind that the children have already spent three days in the forest, abandoned by their parents, and with no hope of finding a way out. But how do they react to the first human voice in such a long time? It doesn't faze them; they are not surprised or astonished or delighted at finding help at last in their plight. Between bites, they reply:

> *The wind so mild,*
> *The heavenly child.*

And cool as cucumbers, they keep eating, unabashed.

That's what they are: egocentrics, never troubled or impressed by anything or anyone. They know only their self-centered needs, to which they cling. Moreover, they tell a lie, both of them this time, albeit, one must admit, quite poetically. Their behavior, however, is not poetic. Hansel, who finds the roof tasty, tears off a large piece, and Gretel knocks out window panes. All of which simply means that they are wrecking the house and smashing the windows.

Not only do they consume only the best (and ignore the bread) without giving it a second thought, but they unhesitatingly destroy someone else's property.

Nevertheless, despite these obvious, even blatant facts, one finds this fairy-tale hero and heroine sweet and dear and as charming as Ludwig Richter and many other illustrators have drawn and painted them.

These are remarkable antitheses. They occur not only in this story.

There are parents who find their children sweet and dear despite facts that point unequivocally to the opposite. Such parents are uncritical of their offspring, and they consider their little darlings the best children in the world. The people around them have a different opinion and find these children unbearable. Some regard them as little monsters, and some would prefer doing something quite horrible to those nasty little brats.

I leave it up to the individual reader: let him do what he likes to them. As a rule, one does not do it; but most people know such children. At the moment, Hansel and Gretel have a thing or two in common with them. They are unrestrainedly relishing the gingerbread house.

But now: out comes the witch.

What is she going to do?

First of all, I have to correct myself. I have jumped the gun about something that has not yet been stated. For you see, no version of the fairy tale explicitly identifies the woman emerging from the house as a witch. I can make this mistake of getting ahead of myself only because I know the plot. Most people, including nearly all children, will react in the same way, for the witch has gained international fame and is depicted in many fairy-tale books as an old, nasty, ugly crone. One can also imagine that she has an ugly voice and giggles hideously.

But the opposite is true. For the story says explicitly that she calls her renowned "Nibble, munch, and crunch" in a *fine* voice.

We are told that she is old, indeed ancient, that she walks with a stick, and that her head waggles. That's all. The Bechstein version even refers to her as *Mütterlein* (little mother).

The children are terribly frightened when she appears, and they have every reason to be, when we recall what they have been doing to her house. However, the old woman does nothing to inspire their fear. She does not threaten or scold them or even reproach them in any way. On the contrary, she actually puts their minds at ease. "No harm will come to you," she says. And what else does she do? She calls them "dear children," amicably invites them to stay, takes them each by the hand, and leads them into the house.

And inside, the good times roll! She bids them come to the table and serves them everything their hearts desire: pancakes with sugar, milk, apples, and nuts, marzipan, (Bechstein version) and delectable cakes. No spinach in her house, no potatoes, no turnips, no cabbage. Absolutely nothing that children don't like; just sweets and goodies.

"Have a good time," she says. And after the delicious meal, she prepares two lovely white "little beds."

The children are not ordered to help with the dishes or to wash themselves or brush their teeth. Not a word.

Hansel and Gretel lie in their fine beds and feel as if they were in heaven.

The friendly crone offers them all these things. There is no trace of a wicked witch in her, and even an adult could envy the children for this heaven on earth. So imagine the reaction of children, at least the children who hear this story for the first time. Here they find a "little mother" who forgives everything, who never scolds no matter what you may do, who offers you a friendly welcome even after you've wandered around the forest for a long time, who has food galore and only the best, who spoils children, serves them, and makes all their wishes come true.

Next to this portrayal, a real mother—no matter how nice and loving she may be—has to pale. No small number of children must prefer this friendly old woman as a mother and be willing to make an exchange.

But before children have a chance to be dissatisfied with their own lives, the fairy tale goes on, nipping such wishes in the bud. The highly attractive old woman is now unmasked as a wicked witch and her alluring gingerbread cottage as cunning bait in a deadly trap. Anyone who goes inside, we are told, is killed by the witch; she boils him and eats him.

This is made clear and will bring most children back to earth again, to hard facts, especially when they have heard the entire fairy tale. Afterward, they will certainly prefer their own mothers again, even if their mothers—the way things are and also have to be—make demands and prohibit this or that. Normally, children are realistic and perceptive, and they grasp such necessities.

Our fairy-tale hero and heroine do not do so. They do not want a normal mother. They are far more demanding, and their demands have already been met. Blissfully and happily they lie in their little white beds. But the story continues, and we will see what happens to them.

The witch gets up early, looks at the two children, who are still "resting sweetly" and have such nice "full, red cheeks." "They'll make a tasty morsel," she mutters—and so much for the children's Never-Never-Land.

The witch grabs Hansel, carries him to a small stable, and locks him up "behind a barred gate." To be sure, she cannot have grabbed him very harshly, for he is still asleep, only waking up inside the stall.

She handles Gretel a lot less gingerly. She keeps shaking her until the little girl wakes up. "Get up, lazybones!" cries the witch, and she orders Gretel to cook good food for Hansel in order to fatten him up. "When he is fat, I'll eat him," declares the witch. Gretel weeps bitterly, but this does not help her. She has to do what the witch demands.

The situation has taken a very unpleasant turn, and the sweet, good, friendly crone suddenly reveals an entirely different face. She has locked up poor Hansel in a stable, and many readers will feel sorry for him. But not quite justifiably. For the boy has provoked what is being done to him here. He deserves what he is getting, for this is precisely what he wanted. All that is happening is that his wishes are coming true very precisely. He is receiving what he wanted and what he yearned for.

Hansel wanted to remain a child, refusing to give up all the pleasant features of this developmental stage. And the fairy tale grants him this privilege. He wants no bread and certainly not a measly little morsel. So he obtains a whole edible house. He wants to do nothing but to be spoiled. And that is what happens. He wants to be fed the very best foods, waited on, and nicely put to bed. He enjoys it all and feels as if he were in heaven.

But wishes have consequences. This morning, Hansel does not even have to walk. He is picked up like a baby and carried. He winds up in a stable and peers through the bars into the world like an infant in a playpen. This is his new outlook. Little children do not need much space to run around in; a few square yards suffice. They do not yearn for freedom as yet; they are still happy in confinement.

But Hansel is no longer an infant, so he reacts differently. He feels pent in, deprived of his freedom, helpless. This is the other side of the coin. He did not want the big forest, so now his existence is restricted to a tiny stable. He did not want to be active, he did not want to act—so he is *acted upon*.

He has gotten his dream mother, who spoiled him, and he has enjoyed all the good things she did for him. But now he is forced to realize that the friendly crone is suddenly showing an entirely different side. She wants to fatten him and then eat him up. This is disastrous, but not undeserved.

It was Hansel who absolutely refused to leave his mother, doing anything he could to remain with her, and managing once to get back to her. The woodcutter's wife was not moved by Hansel's dependency, and she sent him out again. Yet how many mothers are this resolute? They are only human, and devoted sons who need love can obtain a great deal from their mothers. There are any number of very tender and charming little boys who manage to be spoiled and pampered by their mothers in a way that is very close to the witch's treatment of the fairy-tale protagonists here. Such little boys are not unaware, cannot be unaware, of what they are doing. Their behavior can have an extremely serious feedback effect on their mothers. The mothers attach themselves to their children, trying to keep them, refusing to give them up, never letting go if possible.

Our fairy tale depicts this very drastically. The witch locks the boy up, isolating him—from the world—and depriving him of mobility. To make up for it, she cooks him the "best food." And she plans to devour him entirely some day.

These dangers are by no means confined to fairy tales and

fiction. Such a fate is one of the greatest perils in a child's development. Many children suffer what Hansel is threatened with. They are devoured by their mothers—devoured out of love, to be sure. First the son is tied to his mother's apron strings for too long a time; then the mother refuses to let him go. She refuses to do without his love, devotion, and attachment; she "keeps him in"—body and soul, if possible, and systematically. She spoils him, shining his shoes, doing his laundry, ironing his shirts. And she cooks him "the best food," because she knows that the way to a man's heart is through his stomach.

Such mothers only give, asking nothing, living entirely for their children, thus attaching them and hoping that their children will never leave them. Some mothers succeed. But if such a son ever marries, his wife has not the slightest chance in the world of holding a candle to his mother. For the rest of his life, he will be convinced that he was better off with his mother in every way, that she was more understanding, took better care of him, and, needless to say, was a better cook. By his lights, he is right. No wife—however much she may love him–can do for him what his mother did for him. Any other woman can only disappoint him.

Sigmund Freud found that these men have a complex, and he gave it the characteristic name of "Oedipus complex." Oedipus, the hero of Greek mythology, killed his father, albeit unwittingly, and married his mother. Freud imputed similar unconscious intentions to the sons. He reproached them for wanting exclusive possession of their mothers.

This is often the case. Many sons do not want to detach themselves from their mothers; they cling to them, as Hansel does initially, and refuse to grow up. This is a well-known situation, undisputed by psychology.

Less well known is the part that certain mothers play in this drama. Professor Freud said nothing about them. He bashfully concealed what the witch in the Hansel and Gretel fairy tale demonstrates in all clarity. Needless to say, Freud could not expect anyone to accept such an image of motherhood. Who can accuse mothers? Mother love, so often invoked, is sacrosanct in our culture. And it remains sacrosanct even when exaggerated and self-centered maternal love smothers children and leaves them by the wayside as psychological cripples.

Hansel has been frightened so effectively that he would not care to be left by the wayside. He notices just in time that being spoiled leads to loss of freedom and to captivity, and to being eaten up in the end. He does not wish to be eaten up. He finally starts defending himself. His good feelings for the friendly crone disappear. Despite the fine food that he is served daily, he recognizes how dangerous she is to him, and he starts to work out his plan of action.

Every day, the witch steals over to him and calls, "Hansel, stick out your finger so that I can feel whether you will soon be fat." Hansel is cunning and does not do what she asks. Instead of the finger, he sticks out a "little bone." His trick prevents him from being eaten.

Now, this is a very strange scene. In Bechstein's version, the witch tells him to stick *one* finger through the bars, and even less rigorous psychoanalysts will conclude that Hansel's penis, and not his finger, is meant. This may or may not be the case. But one thing *is* conspicuous: the witch does not seem to have such a clear conscience. Why else would she "steal" over to Hansel? After all, she is alone in the house and not responsible to anyone. Equally odd is her sudden dim vision. Her eyes, we are told, are so poor that she cannot make out the bone and mistakes it for Hansel's finger. A short time ago, she could easily recognize the children's "full, red cheeks." Is it possible that she may not care to see what she is now doing and feeling? Is she repressing her wicked erotic thoughts?

There is no doubt, however, that she is checking Hansel.

Unquestionably, one can expect any wickedness of her; but I do not believe that she truly intends to eat him. She is certainly no cannibal, for it has never been customary here, or anywhere else in the world, to devour one's own children. This act is meant symbolically.

That is why she is not interested in how fat Hansel is. She is actually checking his level of development. She wants to know how mature he is. She wants to convince herself that he is no longer an infant. She cannot do anything with infants, for they are neuters. She is waiting for Hansel to finally emerge from his self-centeredness and egocentricity, to turn into a boy and display boyish warmth, affection, and devotion to her. But she is disappointed.

Warned by Gretel, Hansel knows all about the witch's intentions and repels her. Instead of a warm hand, he sticks out a cold, hard bone.

He does what all boys do at some point, what they have to do in order to grow up. They terminate their tender relationship to their mothers, a relationship that has lasted for many years. Their act is not the result of a whim; these boys have outgrown a phase of development.

In fortunate instances, the change occurs imperceptibly for all parties and is virtually taken for granted. This is frequently the case when there are many children in a family. Usually, however, a mother does notice the sudden change in her son's behavior and, if she is very good, she ignores it. Many mothers are chagrined and saddened. Who can blame them? A few mothers will attempt to preserve the old relationship.

And some mothers are totally unwilling to forgo their son's love. These are not necessarily unfulfilled single mothers or mothers of only children. There are many wives who find their good and tender relationship to a son more satisfying than their relationship to their husbands.

A good son loves his mother, recognizes her, and is affectionate and devoted. He listens to her, is helpful, and won't hear anything said against her. He trusts her, shares his worries and problems with her; he talks to her and respects her advice.

Such sons come in all age groups; some have gray temples. All of them are concerned about their mothers and try to do as they ask. Most of them have a bad conscience if they do not come to a meal on time.

That's what sons can be like. They are found in all walks of life. But tell me, please: who knows of husbands with such qualities? They are rare. Even average husbands often show too little concern for their wives, viewing them as some kind of personal property and often becoming unfaithful to them.

An equal number of wives are, consequently, in an unsatisfactory situation, and very few (so far) are willing or able to take the easy way out, as men do and as any number of men regard as their right. Besides, women have different needs. They make different demands. Their wishes and desires cannot, as a rule, be satisfied by a simple "quickie" with someone else.

Some women draw their own inferences from this disagreeable situation. They find a solution that gives them a great deal more than some fleeting lover can give them. At the same time, however, they demonstrate their typically female needs. Their primary goal is not sex. They can do without it, if necessary. They have a more important goal, but one that they cannot attain with their husbands. So mothers get their sons to give them exactly what they need.

Little boys are glad to go along with them. Many promise their mothers to marry them some day, when they are big and can earn a lot of money. All psychoanalytical opinions notwithstanding, this wish has nothing whatsoever to do with sexuality. Little boys love their mothers and express their love with tenderness and affection. Mothers and sons enjoy this, and indeed they should; it is good for both sides.

However, big boys do not keep the promise made by little boys. Big boys want to run away from their mothers. But because they, like nearly all representatives of the male sex, are soft and sentimental in their heart of hearts, it is not difficult for a skillful mother to influence her son and induce him to remain.

Sons are especially susceptible to this influence. Many of them, with no help from their mothers, have a bad conscience when planning to leave home. In fact, a bad conscience seems to be typical of the male emotions. Almost no husband is unfaithful to his wife without remorse. He feels remorseful even when he forgets a wedding anniversary and on many other occasions as well. Women react in this way far more seldom, and mothers who keep their sons attached with all their feminine skill, preventing them from developing any further, have no such scruples. Most of these women even picture themselves as extremely loving mothers because they do so much for their sons.

This is possible only because they are unaware of their own intentions. If reproached for what they are doing, these mothers would indignantly ward off such suspicions, and they would be right in their own terms. Their unconscious behavior makes them so successful, and many sons haven't got a prayer.

As with the witch, their training as "mama's boys" begins with their being spoiled; being spoiled makes them dependent, as we have said. Next, their freedom is taken away. Excellently cared for, they are isolated from other people and cut off from their influences. Stone walls do not a prison make; mothers have subtler but equally effective devices at their disposal. They isolate their sons psychologically. They prevent them from being influenced by others, whether groups of the same age, friends, or a girl. Their boys will go along only with what Mother says, thinks, and believes, and they will be convinced that she wants only what's best for them. Sons almost never doubt a mother's good intentions.

Our fairy tale depicts this condition as wretched captivity, and this is good. With this image, it warns against being "seduced" by mothers. Indeed, the witch's house with all its delights and the tiny stable are images for one and the same thing.

Anyone who sits in a stable, unfree and dependent, and regards his condition as heaven on earth is doomed. He becomes part of his mother—as though he has really been eaten up—and his filial love usually delights her until she is well on in years, walking on crutches like the witch and waggling her head. Skillfully tamed sons are more faithful than many husbands.

Hansel escapes this fate by the skin of his teeth. Ultimately, his trick with the bone does not help him. After four weeks, the witch loses patience. "Fat or skinny, tomorrow I will slaughter him," she says, sealing his doom. No trick can help him now. His possibilities are exhausted; he cannot elude the caldron on his own.

Until this point in the plot, he has been the active one. His actions have determined the events. He strewed pebbles and bread, he suggested the "big feast," he assigned Gretel the sweet window panes. And what has all this brought him? He is doomed, and so is his sister. The witch wants to shove Gretel into the oven. Hansel cannot prevent her from doing so. If no miracle occurs, then he will soon be boiling away on the stove.

A miracle does occur. Gretel, so far inconspicuous and ancillary, takes the initiative. She saves herself and her brother. With unforeseen courage and amazing energy, she shoves the witch into the oven.

This is the first clear indication that the story has two protagonists and that they are amazingly different from each other. This may come as no surprise; for after all, one is a boy and the other a girl. But is this picture correct? Does Hansel act like a typical boy, and are Gretel's actions typical for a girl?

This question certainly cannot be answered in three sentences; it only throws up further questions. For example, is there such a thing as a typical boy or girl? Aside from physical things, what really distinguishes boys and girls, men and women?

The opinions on this issue are numerous and divergent. Nothing is certain, and all we know for sure is that in the Western world women survive men by four or five years. This fact has dealt a hard blow to the theory of the "weaker sex." Nor are other theories any better. They generally depend not on facts, but on the century and the society. Not too long ago, people were convinced that a woman had no soul. In the East, they have no say in anything. In the Soviet Union, they practice all professions; they are locksmiths, architects, or engineers, without further ado.

Nowadays, differences are not talked about as much. Equality is the buzzword, stirring emotions in numerous countries.

Be that as it may, the problem most certainly starts in childhood, right at birth. However, I would discount the possibility of any innate value difference between male and female, and I hope my readers agree with me. Still, one *can* argue about whether there are innate distinctions in behavior.

This is an issue one can only speculate about. But one can investigate the "homemade" differences and ask how fathers and mothers train, program, and influence girlish and boyish conduct.

The witch shows how mothers produce typical boys and typical girls.

Thus, I once again leave the dramatic climax of the story and return to the passage in which Hansel and Gretel stand before the witch's house.

At this point, they are quite plainly children. Nothing indicates any specific gender distinction. They are still alike, and neither child is aware of being male or female. They have quite obviously not yet discovered this difference. And presumably, they would have remained in the stage of their "innocence" for a long time. But they are not permitted to remain innocent. Someone rudely interferes in their life, drastically showing them how different they are from each other. This someone is the witch.

At first, she welcomes the children with open arms, taking Hansel by one hand and Gretel by the other and leading them into the house. Both children are served good food and given nice beds. They are treated with complete equality.

This is consistent with real life. Babies and infants have no sex as far as their mothers are concerned. They are diapered, fed, and put to sleep with the same amount of love. But sooner or later, a change comes about. This change is gradual.

Our fairy tale concentrates this change on the mother's part and brings it about quite suddenly. The next morning, from one instant to the next, the two children turn into a boy and a girl. Their equality is abolished. The witch reacts with extreme vehemence to the sexual difference of the children, treating them accordingly. She picks up the boy and carries him to a stable. Here, he is pampered, spoiled with the finest food. Gretel's experience, however, is entirely different. She is rudely shaken awake and snapped at: "Get up, lazybones." Gretel is then intimidated and pushed around by the witch. She has to get water, start the fire, cook the food, and feed her brother. She has to go out at the crack of dawn and hang up the caldron. She is belittled, says Bechstein, and is fed only crab shells. When she cries, the witch responds, "Stop blubbering. It won't help."

This is how hard mothers bring up their daughters to become hard girls, and one cannot even blame them for preparing girls for life in this way. For many girls, life is truly this narrow. It is restricted to a husband, home, and children; and today as in the past, men still set great store by a nicely run home. A high school or college degree will scarcely improve a girl's chances of marrying; and after all, every daughter is supposed to get a husband. This is the ambition of most mothers, and so they train their daughters toward this goal from early on. Daughters are not supposed to become free, independent human beings—on the contrary. They do not have to be especially intelligent—men are uncomfortable with intelligent women, and thus the latter are less in demand. And on no account can they be proud. A wife is a dependent. She has to be prepared for this condition. Girls have to be trained to become the proper dependents. And the witch painstakingly shoots for this goal.

The task is all the easier for her because she is a woman. No one has unarguably figured out the great significance of gender in rearing children. I myself first realized this problem in "Hansel and Gretel." Here it is quite patent. Obviously the witch would never lift Gretel out of bed and carry her to the stove so that she could start the fire. Only Hansel, the boy, is handled with kid gloves. And the witch also visits him every day. Her daily visit is not necessary for checking purposes. She does not need to touch his hand every day. But she visits him nevertheless. She seeks physical contact with him, daily touching. She would never dream of it with Gretel, who gets to eat only crab shells, after all.

Initially, we identified food (bread) with love. We can make the same equation here. Only Hansel receives good food from the witch.

The idea that the fairy tale expresses here, indeed drastically overstates, is really quite natural. It simply makes a difference that the mother is female and the son male. That the two sexes attract one another is no speculation. This fact is, no doubt, something that nature gives us at birth. And this trait is most certainly not so subtle that one distinguishes between outsiders and family members. The law of the attraction of opposites pays no heed to kinship degrees. Hence, the way a boy loves his mother is necessarily different from the way he loves his father. And a girl's relationship to her father has a different quality than her relationship to her mother. The same holds true for parents. The mother's attachment to her son is stronger—and also different—quite simply because he is of the male sex. That is why there is something special about her affection for him.

Now, this does not mean that mothers generally spoil their sons with the finest food but give their daughters only leftovers. The distinction is not shown that crassly. But there is no question that mothers are more prosaic with their daughters. Furthermore, there are far more touches of hardness, coldness, and nastiness in the female-to-female mother-daughter relationship than in the mother's female-to-male relationship with her son. Traces of such behavior are apparent in the way the witch treats Gretel. This would not be remarkable if similar or comparable patterns were evinced in the male-to-male father-son relationship. But this is not the case. Fathers usually love their sons if for no other reason than that they *are* sons.

We obviously have to seek the cause of this discrepancy in the relationships that women have to one another. These relationships are primarily not as good as the relationships between men. The reason may lie in the centuries of female dependence and lack of self-sufficiency. Women have been able to live only vicariously, through their husbands, and have been unable to get along without them; the husband has had to support his wife and their children.

That is why there has been only one possibility for women: They have had to act through their husbands. Alone, they were nothing, possessed nothing, and were regarded as nothing. If they did not catch a man, they were derided as old maids or bluestockings. So only one goal was left for them: They had to find a husband. No one could help them in this endeavor, least of all other women, who were their rivals. One cannot achieve solidarity with rivals, and one does not like them as a rule.

The male situation is altogether different. Men's relationships with one another are primarily good. Men like one another and enjoy making friends with one another. They have shown solidarity with one another since early history, and they still show solidarity today. They like forming groups, fraternities, fraternal organizations, lodges, orders. They like male conviviality in clubs and bars. And the great male brotherhood unites men in nearly all countries into a certain kind of community: military service. Here, men are comrades, buddies.

Women lack all this. They have not fought together in wars, have not known brotherhood in arms, have not faced danger together while singing, drinking, gambling. The exchange among women, aside from religious orders, has been limited to gossiping at the village well. Nor has much changed in this respect. Today, they chat by stairwells, or else they are suburban wives, left alone all day, but still dependent solely on their husbands.

A good and positive relationship between women is not historically preprogrammed. And a good relationship between men is practically taken for granted. Why this digression? It strikes me as necessary for understanding children, especially girls, and it can help clarify the still-existent belittlement of women.

Only a girl . . .

Why only a girl? A girl is truly disadvantaged, and a girl has a harder time than a boy. The boy has his tender, erotic relationship to his mother, and the mother is around nearly all day long. However, the boy can also have a very good relationship to his father; a good relationship is even customary among men. As a son, he often has the bonus of being the heir apparent, and tender, loving relationships are possible with fathers, too. Nearly all boys romp and roughhouse with their fathers, thus having male-to-male physical contact.

And what does the girl have? She does not have a similar relationship to her mother. What the boy, being male, has as a bonus, the girl, being "only" a girl, has as a minus. All girls resemble Gretel at least slightly.

Needless to say, the daughter's erotic and tender relationship to the father is similar to the son's relationship to the mother. But when is the father ever at home? He has to work. Meanwhile, the daughter is drudging in the kitchen, and the brother is playing in the street. That's the way it is. Unfortunately.

Such a way of life leaves its stamp on children, molding boys in one way and girls in another. In any case, the conditions of their rearing are very different, and it is not surprising that they develop differently, boys as "masculine" and girls as "feminine," but not in the way that most people think. What happens to Gretel shows this very lucidly.

She is pushed around by the witch and treated like a servant. She has a bad time of it and suffers. She cries, but this does not mean that she gives up or breaks down. She is tough, the way most girls are tough. She neither loses heart nor acts heedlessly. She keeps her feelings under control.

Hansel, in this situation, would probably have gotten so furious and desperate that he would have started punching the witch, which would doubtlessly not have helped him very much. Gretel does not do so. But the instant she gets a chance, she acts. Not emotionally and not heedlessly, but rationally and expediently.

She is told to crawl into the oven and check whether the oven is hot enough to put in the bread. But she perceives the witch's true aim. Gretel is not naive: she has an alert (sixth?) sense. She does not fool herself, nor does she fail to see the danger. She realizes that the witch wants to kill her. She deals with the situation realistically, keeping her wits about her, remaining calm and composed, not letting on what she is going through.

I really do not know why women are said to react hysterically in emergencies. It is not true, as experience always proves. Perhaps they get hysterical when they have misplaced their hatpin or car keys. But certainly not in crucial situations. At such times they act, as Gretel does, and they are not passive.

In the incredibly short time that Gretel has, she develops an intelligent and effective plan.

First she pretends to be stupid. "I don't know how to do it," she says. The witch believes her and puts her down as a "silly goose." Then Gretel tricks the witch into demonstrating what she should do. "Show me," she says. "Sit down on it; I'll push you in" (1812 Panzer version). And the witch actually sits down on the oven board.

Thus, the theoretical part of Gretel's plan concludes successfully. Now she has to act—and act decisively. Which she does. Without reflecting for long, she shoves the witch into the oven "as far as she could." Then she "quickly" (1812 Panzer version) shuts the iron door and bolts it. Her plan has worked.

The witch starts howling and burns to death miserably. Gretel is unmoved. She runs to Hansel and joyfully announces, "We are saved! The old witch is dead!" She has actively and successfully terminated the practical part of her plan as well.

I fear that we greatly deceive ourselves about "little girls." This term alone reflects our false notions. We wrongly tend to regard them as only sweet, darling, tender, and perhaps even helpless. They may be all these things *too*, but by no means *only*. They also have a plethora of other qualities, which we often do not ascribe to them, because we do not take girls quite seriously. This attitude has no basis in fact. The opposite attitude would be more correct, for the great challenges that girls have to deal with make them develop special qualities.

Gretel shows the effects her destiny has upon her. First, it turns out that she can think, indeed think very quickly. Her plan is expedient, because it is logical and consistent. And it is original, to boot. The plan she has come up with in such a short time proves that she is imaginative and creative.

Gretel is not stupid. She only pretends she is. She gets away with it; the witch is taken in and calls her a "silly goose." These words are a tribute to Gretel's ability to adjust deftly to a critical situation.

I cannot say to what extent her conduct may be generalized. But I can imagine that men who view women as "silly geese" risk being taken in as thoroughly as the witch was taken in by Gretel.

Gretel proves herself on a practical level as well. She does not hesitate and is not timid. Timidity is anything but a feminine trait. Gretel is courageous and has presence of mind. When she acts, she is decisive, almost cold-blooded, and ultimately ruthless. These are by no means purely masculine qualities.

Hansel would not have succeeded in all this. He would have come to ruin at the very start, for boys cannot take much punishment. Hansel would have climbed into the oven unthinkingly, and he probably would not have had the nerve to kill the witch without giving it a second thought.

Hansel is like many boys, and Gretel is a very typical girl. In its clear and drastic imagery, the fairy tale corrects a widespread prejudice about boys and girls, about male and female. It shows what children are like, perhaps what they are truly like. And we parents are instructed about things that are worth pondering.

Gretel runs to her brother and opens the stable. Hansel leaps forth like a bird from its cage, joyously hugging his sister, and the two children kiss each other.

In the fairy tale, this is a brief sentence, a tiny scene. In point of fact, the two children have taken an important and decisive step in their development. Children who fail to take this step will often suffer for the rest of their lives, because they remain tied to their mother and dependent. Hansel and Gretel have freed themselves. Now that they are saved, they turn to each other, and this is the correct way for them at present. The child-to-child relationship supplants the close attachment to the mother. Focusing on other children, "the street," things outside the home, forms the new dimension. Their infancy is over.

For Hansel and Gretel, infancy ends with their liberation. They have both changed; they now behave differently. They no longer swoop down on goodies. The gingerbread house no longer interests them. They have developed beyond it. Nor are they afraid now. They step into the witch's house, search it, and find their well-deserved reward: pearls and gems. Gretel fills her apron with these valuables. Hansel stuffs his pockets, explaining with newly developed expertise, "These are better than pebbles." He is right. They are also better than bread crumbs. But he is beyond bread crumbs, too. He no longer wants to stand still; he does not want to go back. He wants to go forth, out of the witch's forest. The two start off.

A few hours later, they come to a body of water, which they cannot cross. The road to "new shores" is just not that easy, it demands new abilities, initiative, inventiveness. You are not given anything for free at any point in the development. You have to earn every step forward with your own sweat.

Hansel stands there, looks, and says, "I do not see a plank or a bridge." Disappointed, he concludes, "We cannot get across." This is his contribution to resolving the problem. He is still too demanding. He wants to be waited on, just as he was waited on in the stable. He takes it for granted that there should be a plank or bridge.

Hansel, like so many boys and so many men, is the sort of person for whom bridges must be built, who is constantly thrown back upon (female) help. Few men can get along on their own, and if they do, they often develop odd habits and have a shorter life expectancy.

For the rest of his days, Hansel will remain as helpless as he is in this situation. Without his sister, he would never have gotten to the opposite shore. Gretel has learned that she has to help herself if she wants to get anywhere. She discovers the white duck and says, "If I ask her, she will help us across."

She asks for help. This is entirely different from expecting help. A hard lot makes people modest, and it also makes them inventive and helps them develop new capacities. Gretel can communicate with the duck. It would never have occurred to

Hansel even to try. A girl has possibilities that will always remain alien and incomprehensible to the opposite sex. These abilities sometimes make men unsure of themselves, but they have never thought about it.

Hansel is not surprised that the duck understands Gretel, goes along with what she asks, swims over to the shore, and offers its services. The boy takes the entire incident for granted. It fits his expectations. He does not despair when he is at the end of his rope and does not know where to turn. Someone will help him, he is convinced of this.

And he has every right to be convinced. He will in fact nearly always find someone to take care of him, worry about him, or comfort him, someone who has the ideas that never occur to Hansel. The other sex is programmed for these tasks. Now Gretel helps him, and he registers this without comment. He does not praise her, does not thank her, nor does he let her go first. He takes the lead and sits in the soft feathers of the duck. Egoism is a salient feature in his background.

But now that he is sitting so comfortably, he becomes a gentleman. He asks his "little sister" to sit with him. She is and remains the little girl, notwithstanding everything she has done.

Failing to grasp reality, millions of men call their mate "baby," "doll," and other equally erroneous names. If any sex tends to show childish qualities, it is the male sex.

Hansel's "generous" invitation for Gretel to ride with him is by no means selfless. He will always have to have someone next to him. He may have freed himself from his mother, but he will never forget her. His yearning is released as an energy. All his life, he will yearn for female closeness and warmth. The first thing he did was to hug and kiss Gretel, and now he wants her next to him. He is dependent on attachment and touch. He needs affection, love, and pleasure.

Thus, he wants to have Gretel sit next to him, and he would probably place his arm around her lovingly. But he does not get the chance. Gretel rejects his offer. "The two of us will be too heavy for the little duck," she says. "Let her carry each of us in turn." She has learned this attitude from experience. Her own difficulties and problems help her understand other people. Having suffered herself, she feels sympathy. She has taken care of her brother and liberated him; now she shows concern for the duck. But Hansel shows no such concern; he has not suffered want. His problem was getting too much of a good thing. This has molded his character.

The two children are brought to the opposite shore one by one. And even the larger swan in the Bechstein version transports them quite separately, which is proper.

At a particular stage, this is quite appropriate. Friendship between boys and girls, love, pleasure, and affection, are over and done with. The change is quite sudden, usually occurring when children start school. In earlier times, the sexes were separated in schools for boys and schools for girls. Although this is no longer the case in most countries, little has changed in the situation. Boys learn very fast, mostly from their schoolmates, that they do not play with girls. And if a boy is actually friends with a girl, then he is quickly ostracized and regarded as not being a real boy, as being a sissy. "He hangs out with girls" is a terrible insult for a boy.

Hansel and Gretel reach the opposite shore safe and sound, and the forest becomes more and more familiar to them. Finally, they sight their father's house, run to it, dash in, and embrace their father.

This is now the correct, necessary, and suitable way. Both of them need this relationship and attachment.

Gretel at last finds the tender contact with the male sex, a contact she has earned and needs. Her feminine energy and ability can now develop in her relationship to her father. And Hansel urgently needs the father, the man, the competition. He can now measure his strength against him and learn something very necessary: namely, that he (Hansel) is not always the biggest, the best, and the strongest. Hansel must know his own limits so that later on he will not wreak too much damage with his pleasure-seeking egoism.

The father, in turn, will now have something from his children. They will no longer indolently lie around in their beds. They have brought home precious objects and are pouring them out in the room. "All their worries were over, and they lived together in great joy," we are told.

The mother is dead in the Grimm version, but not in Bechstein's. Be that as it may, she has performed her essential task and is no longer vital.

The story ends with the sentence "My tale is told, a mouse runs bold, whoever catches it can make a fur cap out of it."

I have tried to catch the mouse and make something out of it. A large fur cap? I leave the verdict to the reader.

In the course of my work, I have grown very fond of the two children, and I have learned to understand parents, especially mothers, and even the wicked witch slightly. I am glad about the ending of the story. It is a good ending.

The little hero and heroine have passed all tests and proved themselves. Now they are capable of leading successful lives. This may not put an end to their problems, but they will be able to deal with them. And that, after all, is what counts.

Little Red Riding Hood

The story of a charming little girl who grossly ignores her mother's instructions, disobediently strays from the proper path, very curiously gazes at her grandmother and the wolf, and is unexpectedly eaten up.

FAIRY tale number 26 of the Brothers Grimm is entitled "Rotkäppchen" in German. It begins as follows: "Once upon a time there was a sweet little girl. Anyone who so much as looked at her loved her. . . ." The first line of the fairy tale in Bechstein goes: "Once there was an absolutely darling, charming little slip of a girl."

These descriptions are highly unusual. None of Red Riding Hood's numerous fairy-tale sisters is depicted in this manner. The other girls are beautiful, wondrously beautiful, pious and good, or else wicked, vile, dark, and ugly. They are either immaculately good or else unrestrictedly bad. No other fairy-tale heroine is called a "sweet girl" or a "charming little slip of a girl." Not Cinderella, not the Sleeping Beauty or Little Mary, nor Hansel's sister Gretel.

Little Red Riding Hood is a very special kind of girl, and perhaps that is the reason this story is so well known, not just in German-speaking countries. It is very popular in England and America. And as early as the seventeenth century, adults at the

French court were already enjoying this story, for it was no children's tale; indeed, a number of its versions could not exactly be considered suitable for minors.

Little Red Riding Hood first saw the literary light of day in 1697, when the story appeared in Paris, in Charles Perrault's famous collection of fairy tales.

For the past one hundred and fifty years, Little Red Riding Hood has been Germany's favorite female child. Everyone knows her, even today, and her name instantly conjures up her image: a sweet little girl with nicely combed hair, a clean dress and white stockings, her basket on her arm, and her little red hood on her pretty head. That is how she was shown by many illustrators. Her personal qualities are also instantly evoked: she is sweet, innocent, friendly, and helpful. It was in this guise that Little Red Riding Hood captured the hearts of children. But she also warmed adult hearts like no other little girl. Charles Dickens was so entranced with her that he would have loved to make her his wife. She was "my first love," he wrote.

In the fairy tale, the wolf is entranced with Little Red Riding Hood. But his intentions are far less honorable. He licks his lips and wants to "snap her up" (*erschnappen*). He calls her "my dear, pious child" and "my dear, charming Little Red Riding Hood." He thinks of the girl as a "tender young thing," a tidbit. His thoughts go even further. "Oh, you dearest, appetizing little hazelnut, you—I have to crack you" (Bechstein).

That is the special thing about this fairy tale: Its innocent little heroine arouses erotic desires. Nothing of the sort occurs elsewhere in the *Kinder- und Hausmärchen* (the *Fairy Tales*), which are so decent and moral on the surface. Officially, no eroticism appears in them; it flourishes only secretly, cryptically. But this is not the case in the story of Little Red Riding Hood. Here, you have to make quite an effort to see the wolf's wishes as "harmless" and overlook the heroine's sex appeal. She is instantly presented in these terms and then provided with the emblem giving her her name: the red hood. "The child looked extremely pretty in the hood, and the little girl knew it," says Bechstein. Little Red

Riding Hood is fully aware of the "signaling" effect of her red hood. She loves it so much that she does not want to wear anything else, say the Brothers Grimm and Bechstein; and if we were to take this statement literally, the little girl would have on nothing but her red hood.

This fits in with the image of the heroine, for it is not by chance that the wolf wants to "snap her up." And something must have induced Charles Dickens to say that Little Red Riding Hood brought him "perfect bliss." For all her innocence, Little Red Riding Hood turns men on.

She is just as sweet and darling as she is vain; and without any doubt, she is still a real child, self-confident, self-assured, and adventurous. Yet, for all her ignorance, she is also a little female.

Some girls show no signs of such behavior. This has nothing to do with how feminine they are. Occasionally, sisters are completely different in this respect: one is decent and proper, the other a little vamp.

Often, birth order is a decisive factor in these differences. First-born daughters are very seldom little femmes fatales. Lots of help and little coquetry are expected from them. They have obligations at an early age and must assume responsibility. That is why these girls tend to be realistic and endowed with common sense.

When a little girl is a spoiled only child, the assumptions made about her are altogether different, and she tends to show feminine charm a great deal earlier. Little Red Riding Hood has no brothers or sisters.

In any case, childhood sex appeal is not innate. It is "man-made." Fathers provoke it, because they are stuck on their little daughters; and some mothers want to have a "sweet girl" and make sure they get one. It is the parents who offer this role, and most little girls gladly take it on. They are typecast in the part and they enjoy it.

The second line of the fairy tale reveals who offers Little Red Riding Hood this part: her grandmother. It is she who gave the little girl the cape of "red velvet." She is willing to give her anything, we are told, and to do anything for her granddaughter. She loves the girl "more than anything," and she is without a doubt a key figure in the plot. But for the grandmother, nothing would have happened; Little Red Riding Hood would have neither strayed nor been eaten by the wolf.

The grandmother merits a detailed study. It turns out that we know very little about her. She loves Little Red Riding Hood and spoils her. Beyond that, the picture of the grandmother is pale and indifferent. We do not learn what she is like or what other qualities she has. We know so much about the wolf and hear so much about the mother in the few lines in which she appears. The grandmother never achieves a profile.

And there are other odd things about her. How many grandmothers live far from the village, half an hour inside the forest, away from the community? And all alone to boot? This is quite improbable.

And there is something strange about her illness. One might send cake and wine to a convalescent; but this is no suitable diet for an illness, whatever it may be.

Nor does the grandmother herself claim to be sick. When the wolf knocks on the door, she calls, "Just turn the knob. I am too weak and cannot get up." Is she merely feeble?

In the Bechstein version, the mother says, "Grandmother is sick and weak and cannot come to us." If Grandmother is not sick, then the mother should merely say that she is "weak." Is she weak?

Rather than run the risk of offending her and suspecting her of bad things, I have to say something about the technique of fairy tales. Fairy tales occasionally use a trick that can otherwise be found only in dreams. This trick consists of presenting a character in a twofold manner; more precisely, personifying him or parts of his personality. The grandmother is such a "part," and this is why she seems so pallid. She is not a complete person, only an aspect of the mother. She embodies certain secret and taboo wishes of the mother's. These wishes do not fit into the community; that is why the grandmother lives far away from the village, in an area to which, normally, outsiders are exiled. Moreover, her activities there are kept secret. No one is to know that she enjoys wine and cake and fails to keep her door locked. And certainly no one must learn that she invites the wolf in. Yet this is precisely what she does.

Granted, the wolf pretends to be Little Red Riding Hood. This is the kind of trick that the seven little kids fell for in "The Wolf and the Seven Young Goats." But would an experienced grandmother fail to recognize the big wolf when he shows up in Little Red Riding Hood's clothing?

I am afraid that the grandmother knew who was at her door. She was truly weak and wanted what happened to her to happen. She let herself be eaten by the wolf. It did not hurt her. It even turned out to be useful for her. Bechstein says that afterward she again became "fresh and healthy."

The separation into grandmother and mother shows the dichotomy within the mother: She is worried about her daughter and is afraid that something could happen to her in the woods. Yet this is the very thing that the mother wants for herself. She would like to be "picked up" and courted, just as Little Red Riding Hood is. The mother would like to hear such friendly words and lovely compliments and receive a visit in the lonely house far from the village. Some people might be indignant at a mother's having such wishes, and that is why these desires are so carefully concealed in our fairy tale; they are camouflaged in a grandmother, who is beyond good and evil for everybody. These are no mothers. These are human beings with human needs. It is conceivable that our fairy-tale mother needs her wishes because she is lonely, lonely as a woman. A man is mentioned only very peripherally in this story. He, the (good) hunter, appears only once, very briefly, and then goes his way again. He does have a rifle, but he does not use it.

Since people are rarely satisfied by wishes, the mother seeks some more tangible route. No direct one, however; she cannot and must not. Yet she does find one through Little Red Riding Hood, although it naturally brings no fulfillment, but only unreal, vicarious satisfaction. We shall see.

The mother is not conscious of her solution. And if it were pointed out to her, she would rightfully deny such an insinuation. On a conscious level, she is quite different. This is shown in the next scene. There are no wishes or fantasies here—just everyday life, the solid upbringing of everyday life. The mother gives her daughter clear instructions. The little girl is told to bring cake and wine to her grandmother. The mother adds some advice about the errand. Her advice is far less clear, and one really has to quote the mother verbatim. Little Red Riding Hood's mother says the following: "Start out before it gets hot, and when you are out, walk decently and do not leave the path, or you will fall and break the glass, and Grandmother has nothing. And when you enter her home, do not forget to say good morning, and do not look around in all the corners."

Yes, here it is! We have to go into detail in order to understand and appreciate these pedagogical methods. "Start out before it gets hot." One honestly wonders what this means, for Little Red Riding Hood is all set to leave; she is standing in front of her mother with her basket on her arm. The mother's admonition would make sense only if she were waking up the child or if they were having breakfast. Her words might then induce the girl to hurry and get going before the midday heat. But in this situation, her words are such as to pressure the girl. In any case, the mother's conduct is not very friendly. She nags her, whether for lack of consideration or on principle, or with some specific goal in mind. Nagging does not raise a child's self-confidence; it makes a child insecure and certainly does not help the child develop independence. It is meant to make children behave nicely, in order to make things easier for the parents.

The mother goes on: "Walk decently."

One must first ask how the child construes this sentence. In all likelihood, she has no precise notion of what is meant. At most, she vaguely senses the aim of this demand; but she does not understand the nebulous instruction. Nonetheless, in this situation, she does not do what she normally does when she fails to understand something: she does not ask what is meant.

This is a frequent behavior of children in areas having to do with morality, sexuality, and reproduction. They do not ask the parents—they remain silent. But as a rule, this does not mean that they know everything or that they are not interested in these matters. Quite the contrary: these themes are usually attractive and exciting for children and are often intensely discussed by them. However, they do not ask their parents. They seldom did so in the past; and even today, after the wave of sexual enlightenment, children do not ask spontaneous and trustful questions about sex any more frequently. Why? Because children have a fine sense of the emotions felt by adults. Their empathetic powers are far greater than ours. They may not be aware of this, nor do they think about it; but they do react. They remain silent because they sense how embarrassing such questions are for us.

They are right. Such questions *are* embarrassing for us. Nor should we pretend otherwise. Someone may doubt this, and he may be right. But just imagine Little Red Riding Hood not listening to her mother's tirades in devoted silence and instead asking amiably, "Mommy, what does 'walk decently' mean?"

Would this not be the very behavior that we try to bring about with our pedagogical methods? Do we not want children to ask questions of their mothers openly, freely, and trustfully? But could we really deal with the situation? Could we be equally free, open, and relaxed about answering? For most of us the issue is quite academic because our children, considerate as they are, normally spare us such questions. And in reality, Little Red Riding Hood would never dream of acting in this way; nor does she do so.

But let's pretend she *has* asked and that the mother is forced to reply. She would have to answer the question amiably, confidently, and in a way that the child would understand; she could not beat around the bush. Fine, let her answer in this way. She would have to say more or less the following: " 'Walk decently' means don't arouse men by wiggling your behind. You shouldn't do this because otherwise you might draw lecherous looks."

Sounds good, doesn't it? But this is where the difficulties start, for now the intelligent daughter will want to know what "arouse" means and what "lecherous looks" are. I cannot help sympathizing with parents who have qualms about such open sexual enlightenment. And speaking of sexual enlightenment, I must reproach the authors of the many books on teaching children the facts of life: these authors oversimplify the problem. It is not easy to answer a child's questions. It's even harder to talk naturally and spontaneously to our children about sex and intercourse. Even a simple question about the sexual organs causes us problems, because there are no natural and spontaneous words for the organs. The very word "intercourse" is unsuitable enough. "The street" is much better oriented in such things. It has hundreds of accurate terms. No wonder, for people talk about sex in the street. At home, we hold our tongues in embarrassment. Sex is freely discussed neither in the middle-class parlor nor in the working-class kitchen. If ever "such things" are brought up, they are frequently mentioned in the way that Little Red Riding Hood's mother tries to touch on the matter.

She has a very good reason to talk about it, for she is worried about her daughter; she senses the danger the girl is in and would like to warn her. Nevertheless, she does not succeed in speaking about it openly. She does not enlighten the girl, she does not even inform her, and thus she cannot prevent the disaster. She does not do the sensible and expedient thing: namely, enlighten Little Red Riding Hood about the character and intentions of the wolf. She gives her daughter no tips or advice on how to conduct herself with the wolf. She does not even dare pronounce the word "wolf."

Little Red Riding Hood remains unenlightened and unprepared, and therefore she blunders her way into the trap, naive and unsuspecting. The mother refrains from doing anything but voicing utterly incomprehensible warnings: "And do not leave the path, or you will fall and break the glass."

An experienced adult may sense that the mother means not the forest road to Grandmother's house, but the "right path," from which the child should not stray. However, an adult is bound to wonder about the second part of the warning. Why glass? he will ask, for Little Red Riding Hood has a bottle of wine in her basket, not a glass. And the adult reader will not understand why such a big girl has to be warned about falling, as if she were a three-year-old.

Only a trained psychologist will catch the mother's drift. He can translate her words into plain language, and the rendering would be as follows: Stay on the right path, or you'll lose your innocence and you'll be a fallen girl.

This is the point the mother is trying to make, this is where her fears lie, and she has good reason to be afraid that something might happen to her daughter in the woods. She ends her catalogue of warnings with the words "And when you enter her home, do not forget to say good morning, and do not look around in all the corners."

She thus changes the subject, retreating to her position as a mother aware of her responsibilities and teaching her child the proper deportment.

The mother's pedagogical approach, as depicted here, fairly corresponds to what many parents practice. They believe that their moralizing will keep their children out of harm's way and protect especially the girls from jeopardizing their morals. Their pedagogical goals are to bring up obedient, well-behaved children. Independence and initiative are regarded less as virtues than as perils. Parents are also skeptical about knowledge, aside from school knowledge. That is why they avoid any further information and evade curiosity. They hope that ignorance will keep their children blissful. Often—as in our fairy tale—their hopes are in vain.

Nevertheless, such pedagogical measures are sometimes successful, and children react positively to the moral appeals of their parents. Such parents are very happy, simply delighted, when their children virtuously promise, "I will do everything properly," and even give them their hand on this promise, as Little Red Riding Hood does.

However, such parental delight is premature. These parents underestimate how well children can conform. Children often sense very accurately what is expected of them, and they often go along with it. Usually, they benefit from their response when their parents are delighted at their behavior.

Little Red Riding Hood no doubt feels how important the topic is to her mother, for the child reacts and ostentatiously gives her hand, in order to lend more weight to the promise. But in so doing, she absolutely fails to react to the meaning of the maternal appeal. The child is neither touched nor impressed by it. She has simply conformed on the outside and will forget everything a moment later. Subsequently, she does not hesitate for even an instant to follow the wolf into the forest.

Words do not influence children. Phrases neither guide them nor change them nor educate them. Of crucial importance is the kind of relationship that fathers and mothers have with their children. It is this relationship that largely molds a child's behavior. The mother's specific relationship with Little Red Riding Hood is the girl's destiny. Nothing would have happened to the child if . . .

But now I have to go back a little.

We have neglected the fact that the grandmother does not really exist. This means that she cannot have given the child anything. Hence, the presents and the red cape come from the mother. It is she who also spoils the daughter. She dresses her "nicely" and provides her with erotic emblems. The mother thus makes the daughter vain, and she is responsible for the child's sensual charisma.

What does the mother get out of all this?

Well, she is in a rather bad situation. Her wishes do not come true, and she cannot achieve anything whatsoever when it comes to sex appeal. The deployment of feminine charms is tolerated only before marriage; they were—and in many places still are— legitimate only as a means of catching a husband. Once a girl has gotten her man, then so much for her feminine charms; and her own husband will not be the last to protest against any kind of female coquetry.

However, the mother has a daughter, a part of herself, perhaps a young image of herself. The mother identifies with her, and anything the mother may not experience is delegated to the daughter. Thus, the mother dresses the daughter in an attractive way, turning her into a "sweet girl." Naturally, she is not conscious of what she is doing. She simply does not realize what her actions involve. Nevertheless, the daughter must sense what is expected of her. Here, even the mother's unconscious wishes have a stronger influence on a child than any words could ever have.

Little Red Riding Hood accepts the part. Her impact on other people is that of a coquettish and womanly yet childlike and innocent little girl: they all find her sweet, charming, darling. At the start of the tale, we are told that everyone liked her and that is what the mother is after; for she probably hears compliments from all sides, she is delighted to hear them, and she unconsciously applies them to herself.

I am not claiming that this is how all little child-females come into being. But some *are* created in this way. Their dissatisfied, frustrated, and sometimes perhaps also unhappy mothers turn them into such persons. The part accepted by such a daughter is, as a rule, learned quickly and then becomes a habit. Most of these daughters play the part all their lives. They will always be intent on arousing other people's interest, drawing their attention, and hearing their compliments.

What many people regard as the character of these women or even as their innate qualities are actually acquired patterns of behavior, created by mothers who suffered some kind of deprivation and sought comfort in their daughters.

But now the mother is worried, specifically worried about her daughter; for Little Red Riding Hood is not going through the village, which would delight the pastor, the mailman, or the grocer's wife. The child is going into the forest. And that is the home of the world-renowned wicked wolf. The wolf will not be content to voice polite compliments, and the mother knows it. However, her child has no inkling of all this. Unsuspecting, innocent, and simultaneously sexy, she will provoke the wicked beast, the mother thinks to herself.

The wolf is no fantastic figment, pale, colorless, and ultimately as unreal as the grandmother. The wolf is a fact, an image, that everyone knows and that many people fear. Little Red Riding Hood's mother is not the only person who would warn people about the wolf. Many mothers would do their best to protect their daughters against the wolf. The fathers of little girls are just as scared of him, the pastor gives sermons against him, and the priest listens to the confessions of those who have fallen victim to the wolf. Now, the wolf may not be the Devil, but he is certainly a relative of his, and mothers, fathers, and men of the cloth are right in warning against him. The wolf is dangerous.

So they say. But I would submit that he is dangerous only because so many people think of him as dangerous and keep warning others about him. Nevertheless, he is a remarkable figure.

He is now waiting to make his entrance. So let me return to the story. Our little girl enters the forest, alone and unprotected, and there he is, the big, bad wolf. Several unexpected things instantly occur.

First of all, the beast does not viciously bare his fangs. Instead, he courteously says, "Good day, Little Red Riding Hood." Who would have thought?

And how does our heroine react to the wild animal, whose name the mother did not even dare pronounce? Does the little girl scream when he appears, does she panic, is she shaken with horror, paralyzed with fear? Nothing of the kind. She amiably returns his greeting. That's all. No, not quite. She says, "Thank you, *Wolf*." She actually knows the wicked animal's name.

One would not think it possible, but such things happen frequently. Parents who are racking their brains—"How shall I tell my child?"—will often come to realize that the little daughter or son whom they consider innocent and unsuspecting is very well informed about the things that the parents have carefully prepared themselves to tell him in meticulously chosen words.

Parents should not be alarmed when they misjudge their children. The reason is that children at a very early age have their own realms, which we do not know. These realms encompass their friends, the group of children they socialize with. We scarcely have a chance to find out what goes on here. We know little about their relationships and practically nothing about their conversations. In any event, both love and death are already topics in kindergarten, and the little children are extremely realistic and unsentimental in regard to both areas.

This is how Little Red Riding Hood acts toward the wolf. She doesn't bat an eyelash, and she has a friendly conversation with the animal. Even more: she conducts herself in a sophisticated way with the big wolf. She is self-confident and independent, thereby appearing in a completely new role. She is absolutely no longer the obedient girl who listened to her mother's instructions.

The original description of the heroine as a dainty, well-behaved little girl turns out to be false here. Her daintiness at best corresponds to the role that she plays for her mother. And Little Red Riding Hood is anything but well behaved, for she ignores what her mother tells her to do. The child does not waste a single thought on the strict warnings; and without further ado she breaks her solemn promise. She shows no trace of a bad conscience.

The child's reaction is certainly not due to any lack of forcefulness on her mother's part. Her mother is quite firm. No one can doubt her pedagogical competence or her authority. Certainly not the mother herself. She is quite convinced of her authority and issues her instructions from a position of power. Her words may be hazy and confused, but the standards and convictions behind them are unequivocal. The mother must rightfully assume that Little Red Riding Hood knows what she is driving at, and she cannot doubt that her daughter will behave accordingly.

Many mothers who raise their children in a similar fashion are equally convinced of the success of this pedagogical style. After all, the tradition is centuries old, during which time it has been regarded as the only correct and only successful way of rearing children.

Almost throughout this period (the fairy tale is that old), Little Red Riding Hood has shown the limits of such pedagogical optimism. She clearly demonstrates that the faith of so many parents in the obedience and good behavior of their offspring may be terribly naive. And the conduct of our fairy-tale heroine is certainly no isolated example. Indeed, it is quite typical.

For generations, children have done what Little Red Riding Hood does in the story: They have dutifully said yes and then acted by their own lights. This is how children react if they have no say in the matter. They arrogate the elbow room that they are not granted. Behind the external appearance of obedience and good deportment, they lead their own lives, experimenting and, like Little Red Riding Hood, gathering their own experiences. Because their own experiences involve a greater degree of risk and are gathered against the resistance and despite the prohibitions of grownups, they require energy and forcefulness. Children train their strength in such experiences, maturing and developing character. If this were not so, the majority of children who have undergone an authoritarian upbringing would wind up as adults without color or character. But this is not the case.

The fairy tale touches upon a stickier issue here. In the person of the heroine, with whom, after all, every child identifies, the story advocates highly illegitimate actions and modes of conduct for children—illegitimate, in any case, from a parental point of view. Little Red Riding Hood, a model and positive example for all children, disobeys, breaks promises, launches into questionable and morally dubious adventures, and displays a totally unsuitable curiosity. What if she set a precedent? What if children not only listened enthusiastically to the fairy tale, but also emulated Little Red Riding Hood's behavior? What if they became less obedient and less well behaved, more curious and adventurous and, like our heroine, ignored all-too-restrictive parents?

If Little Red Riding Hood were to make such an impact, then she would indeed be more than a sweet, charming thing. She would be carrying a large amount of social tinder under her apron (or wherever). For if this were the case, the lovely little girl would be rattling away at the foundations of the traditional hierarchy, in which parents command and determine and children obey.

Needless to say, the fairy tale cannot admit such revolutionary tendencies. If it did allow them to enter, no adult would ever tell the story to a child. For who would care to dig a grave for his own authority? Hence, the story shows unequivocally that the heroine's misdeeds lead her to disaster. By way of punishment and as a deterrent for everyone else, the little girl is eaten by the wolf.

This is where the French version ends; and after this unhappy ending, every child ought to regard Little Red Riding Hood's high-handed actions as extremely dangerous.

In all other versions, the heroine is saved; but to prevent any child from so much as thinking that it would be an attractive idea to leave the road, the fairy tale has Little Red Riding Hood regret her misconduct and vow never to disobey her mother again.

As if that were not enough, the Brothers Grimm go further and attach a second version to their tale. This version retells the story, but this time properly and suitably. The heroine does not even entertain the idea of disobeying her mother. She keeps her promise and turns the wolf a deaf ear. She finds him wicked and does not deviate one step from the road.

Thus, the world is orderly again, and any possibility of igniting an explosive is adequately prevented.

Or is'nt it?

The appended story, in my opinion, will contribute little to such safety. It will not correct the original, for hardly anyone is familiar with this addendum, though it is found in every complete edition of Grimms' fairy tales, including the original one. But this version simply lacks charm. So much proper deportment is vapid and boring. This sort of heroine is uninteresting. Red Riding Hood did not become famous for being obedient and well behaved; quite the contrary. And as for the incendiary matter: For two centuries, nothing happened. But then, quite unexpectedly, there *was* an explosion. Suddenly, a younger generation that had been quite indifferent and conformist went to the barricades. We witnessed it. A younger generation grew angry and rebelled, slamming its demands on the table in the face of a terrified bourgeois society. These young people wanted to release us from the constraints of philistine morality. For children, they demanded an end to suppression by parents, school, and government. For themselves, they demanded the right to individuality, their own lives, satisfaction of drives, the elimination of repression, frustration, achievement pressure, and a sexual enlightenment free of any taboo.

At first, during the sixties, some people may have laughed at such extremism. But they did not have the last laugh, for they underestimated these young people. Today, we find democratized upbringing and liberated children everywhere.

Little Red Riding Hood nowadays is no longer "a darling, charming slip of a girl," liked by everyone. She is self-assured and deals with adults freely and unsubdued. She doesn't give a damn about their opinions and views; she prefers orienting her behavior by that of her peers. She does not regard good behavior as necessarily a virtue, and she considers obedience a weakness. She advocates her rights courageously, goes her own way at an early age, and takes the Pill at sixteen. She meets the wolf at parties, and she has done away with the stork.

Reformers laud this development as progress. They wanted active and self-assured children. But they also wanted peaceful and tolerant children. The latter goal, I am afraid, has not quite been reached—nor have a few other goals.

As never before in the past, children now terrorize one another. They envy one another's property, and the more they get, the more dissatisfied they are. They are neither happy nor cheerful, and instead of being charming, they are aggressive. Few of them have a sense of humor, and they are tolerant chiefly toward their own failings.

In no way are they similar to our fairy-tale heroine, who has gained such worldwide popularity. Many of these children resemble the nagging mother and, thus, the representative of the system that the reformers are so passionately fighting against. It happens so frequently: extremes meet. And, as often happens, they have failed to bring about an ideal that was developed and advocated so vehemently. Indeed, no one has ever succeeded in this respect.

Nevertheless, the angry young people were right. They brought a fresh wind into society and new impulses into education. This was necessary. The kind of child-raising principles practiced by Little Red Riding Hood's mother were antiquated and had to be replaced or at least rethought. And as for our present-day youth, even in the so-called good old days, juvenile gangs fought bloody street battles, and children have never been what the old, charming illustrated storybooks tried to make us think they were. Furthermore, nearly every generation has complained and lamented about the evils of young people. The ancient Greeks were already doing so. Two thousand years ago, wise Socrates pointed out: "Today's youth loves luxury. These young people have bad manners, they scorn authority, have no respect for their elders, and spend their time chitchatting instead of working. Young people no longer stand up when their elders enter a room. They contradict their parents, blab their heads off in society, devour the sweets at a table, cross their legs, and tyrannize their teachers." But whatever the old may have thought about the young, every younger generation has turned into useful adults. And our boys and girls can hardly be an exception.

Nevertheless, I would enjoy returning to the sunny forest and the two disparate characters, the little girl and the big, bad wolf. The two of them get along famously. The wild animal proves friendly and amiable, he behaves like a gentleman, and Little Red Riding Hood chats. Apparently, all's right with the world.

But naturally, it's not. The wolf's friendliness is, of course, nothing but a strategy, and the naive child falls for it. His second question already shows his true aims. His polite pretense merely conceals vile lechery. No sooner have the two exchanged their first civilities than the wolf asks bluntly, "What are you carrying under your apron?"

It is quite obvious that the basket of cake and wine cannot be hidden under the girl's little apron. Nor is the wolf interested in this. He's after what's really under the apron. And he aims at it with pointed curiosity—only to meet with a brush-off. Little Red Riding Hood does not react to his hint. In the original version, she fails to hear the question and goes on with the conversation by responding to his first question about where she is going: "Grandmother is sick and weak, so I am bringing her cake and wine; we did our baking yesterday." Elegant, isn't she? Deftly and tactfully, the little girl skirts the issue.

According to the Brothers Grimm, she says that she has cake and wine under her apron, which is obviously not true, hence obviously a pretext. Whatever her reaction may be, Little Red Riding Hood diverts the wolf from his goal. He gives up his gross and direct effort at moving in on her. The skillful little girl scores a point against the big, bad wolf.

The question is, did she really catch his drift? I believe she did. Otherwise, she would have asked him what he meant or she would have naively replied, "I have a dress under my apron." I believe that she is playing the unsuspecting innocent.

Who, however, would actually ask a little girl such a question! Who would reveal this kind of curiosity and this sort of interest? The person asking such a question is no wolf, nor is he threatening or wicked. Little boys ask questions like this one, children of the same age as our heroine. They are profoundly interested in what little girls look like "down there"; and if a little boy goes about it in the right way, many little girls are quite willing to show him what is hidden under their aprons: indeed, they themselves are equally curious to see what little boys have to offer down there.

But anyone as grossly blunt as the wolf does not stand much of a chance. The more elegant path to this goal is by way of a game. This is hinted at in the Bechstein version. Little Red Riding Hood herself gives the cue. "You must be a doctor," she says. The wolf does not go along with her. Nor can he. Playing doctor is taboo, even in a fairy tale, of course.

For parents, playing doctor is problematical. Many parents would rather not hear about it, and quite a few believe that their children never do play doctor. Most parents are fooling themselves. This curiosity is as old as mankind. Ever since Eve put on a fig leaf in Paradise, men have wanted to peek behind it. This curiosity starts at a very early age and never really stops. But it *is* disapproved of.

That is why our fairy tale has no charming little boy, such as we would find in reality; instead, we get a foul and nasty wolf. The moral is obvious: Everything having to do with sex is wicked, beastly, and as hideous as the wolf. Even playing doctor.

Yet these games are well known and widespread in every generation of children. They are not even sexual in the true sense of the word. In any case, many of the children who play doctor are not aware of this side of the game.

Adults are extremely dichotomous in judging these childhood activities. The official positions vacillate between rejecting such games as sinful, vile, and filthy and tolerating them amiably. In between are the adults who regard them as unimportant, unessential, and not worth bothering about.

"Forbidden games" are by no means unimportant for children, for these games offer them a chance to satisfy their curiosity. No enlightenment, however good, can offer such a fine illustration. Neither the loveliest words nor the most graphic pictures can substitute for reality. Besides, reality is a lot more exciting.

Adults hoped that sensible sex education would make such games superfluous and knock the bottom out of childhood curiosity; but these hopes have not come true. How could they? The advocates of sexual enlightenment overlooked something very important: the schizophrenic role that adults play in regard to a child. The dichotomy of adults cannot be bridged, and thus they are faced with an insoluble problem: they are supposed to provide their children with precise verbal explanations for the very things that the parents conceal and gloss over every day and in every way. And not only in regard to their children. We hid our love lives from everyone, and especially from our "innocent" children.

Most children know of kisses only as unerotic rites of greeting. We often avoid even simple affection in front of them. We never caress when they are around, we never cuddle, nor do we touch upon the topic of love in words. And for centuries, the best-kept secret of parents has been the fact that they sleep together. We avoid anything that might hint at our love attachment in this respect.

Our intentions may be good, but we parents should not imagine that we could make our children believe that we form an asexual partnership for bringing up our offspring. Children will refuse to believe that this is our role. Although unenlightened, Little Red Riding Hood did not believe this; and our daughters will believe it even less.

How carefully Little Red Riding Hood's mother tried to keep the secret of the wolf, and how certain she must have been that her little daughter was still completely innocent and unsuspecting! But the mother was deluding herself—as many mothers do. The fairy tale proves it: The little girl not only knows the wolf and greets him in a friendly way, she knows even more. She gives him precise directions for getting to (Grand)Mother's house: "Her house is under the three big oak trees, The nut hedges are below." And now it comes: the child casually adds, "You must know that." So she knows about the wolf's visits; she presumably senses that (Grand)Mother sets great store by his visits. The little girl knows the adult's secret.

We should not underestimate our children's prescience and intuition (or whatever it is). Yet on the other hand, what can happen if they learn the secret? Little Red Riding Hood is quite realistic as well as cooperative in this area. She even sends the wolf to the house. Girls, as a rule, have nothing against their mothers' having sex.

But the wolf will not be sent away. He wants to get at or even under the little girl's apron, for he is lechery personified. Everything else is hypocrisy. Little Red Riding Hood and the grandmother are nothing for him but "tidbits." All his fine-sounding words merely serve this one purpose: he wants to eat them, both of them. He has no qualms; a female can be young and tender or old and wrinkled—so long as she's a female.

None of this daunts our heroine. She and her apron remain untouched. She successfully keeps the wolf aloof on the fine line between courtesy and reserve. Fearless and friendly, she chats with him, never compromising herself. She also listens to him and looks around when he asks her to do so. For is he pointing at anything bad? "I believe," he says, "you don't even hear the little birds singing so sweetly. You walk along as if you were going to school, and it is so delightful out in the woods." So Little Red Riding Hood opens her eyes and suddenly sees the sunlight dancing to and from among the trees and the wealth of beautiful flowers. She does not stop to think; she runs merrily into the forbidden forest and picks a huge bouquet for her grandmother.

Yes, this is the kind of experience you can have with girls: on the outside, they appear obedient and well behaved; they politely make promises—but never keep them. They remain astoundingly immune to parental notions of morality, and, while pretending to conform, they do what they want to do. However, as in Little Red Riding Hood's case, they are not really being malicious or rebellious or defiant, they are simply guileless, and such situations seem to be quite natural and par for the course so far as they are concerned. They are unaware of doing anything wrong, nor are they haunted by any qualms.

Some fathers may pull out their hair because of such "female morality," and their daughters cannot hope for any sympathy, for men, as a rule, cannot understand such behavior. The reason is that men are unfamiliar with it, because they are different and, as boys, they were different.

Certainly, they broke promises, just like Little Red Riding Hood, and disobeyed their mothers. But they at least had bad consciences, and some of these boys were even ashamed.

None of this so much as occurs to Little Red Riding Hood, nor is she a helpless, vulnerable creature. She is more independent and self-sufficient than one generally assumes little girls to be, and she is not easily led astray (in any sense of the word). She did not let the wolf talk her into anything; she ran into the forest of her own free will, and her action was not even thoughtless or heedless. To be sure, her considerations were not moral so much as practical. She told herself, "It is so early in the day that I am sure to arrive on time." It is only after this rational reflection that she launches into the new adventure, looking for flowers, getting deeper and deeper into the woods, but not encountering any danger. When she has picked as many flowers as she can carry, she starts off to her grandmother's house. She is not worried about going the wrong way or not finding the road back.

The wolf, suddenly abandoned by Little Red Riding Hood, has to resign himself to doing without the "tender young thing" for now. She would—he reflects—have tasted a lot better than the old woman. So he decides to make do with the grandmother and heads straight for her home.

He thinks of her as "the old woman," and in German, *die Alte* is a common expression for one's wife. Conceivably, a conjugal scene is about to take place. This would mean that both are renouncing: he renounces Little Red Riding Hood, and she renounces the dream lover.

Be that as it may, this is not very important so far as the heroine is concerned. It is obvious that something sexual is taking place in the remote house, far from the village; and in the eyes of the heroine, this something must be her parents' sex life, which is rigorously shrouded in secrecy.

A number of things would point in this direction.

The wolf knocks and is welcomed. His masquerade as Little Red Riding Hood can, I feel, be overlooked. It masks the sexual content, as is customary in our society and necessary in children's fairy tales.

In the Grimm version, the (Grand)Mother responds to his knocking as follows: "Just turn the knob." This sounds harmless enough. In Bechstein, she calls, "Reach down through the hole in the door, that's where the key is." In the French version, she says, "Give the little peg a pull, then the little stick will fall and the door will open up." Her response would make it appear quite improbable that she is expecting her granddaughter.

The wolf enters and does not even say good morning. He does not come up with his usual friendly words, and certainly not the lovely and seductive ones that he employed with Little Red Riding Hood. Indeed, he says nothing; without uttering a word, he goes over to the bed and swallows the grandmother. He must have first pulled off her nightgown, for he then slips into it himself.

It is clear that no lover behaves in this fashion. But since the wolf—as we have sound reason to conjecture—is not a wicked burglar, there is only one possible solution: he is the husband. Only veteran husbands, as it were, can practice such a terse, loveless, mechanical form of sex.

The image of eating, which the fairy tale chooses here, fits in with the notions of many children. Sexuality is alien to them, and they very frequently associate it with aggression, violence, and struggle.

For our heroine, a secondary detail is important in this scene: the door has remained open. This is explicitly mentioned by the Brothers Grimm and Bechstein; and both versions portray Little Red Riding Hood as being very surprised at finding everything open, "since normally the grandmother prefers to keep herself under lock and bolt," as Bechstein adds.

Easy to understand. This remote area is kept locked by parents, who make sure that the children never enter or even catch a glimpse of the inside. But accidents do happen. Like here. Little Red Riding Hood enters the cottage, which should have been locked; she is surprised, says good morning, but receives no answer. There is nothing to see, and we do not know what she suspects or hears. In our version (Grimm), she thinks, "My goodness, how frightened I feel today," and she finds the situation odd. Bechstein says: ". . . her young little heart felt very frightened."

The obvious thing for the uncertain and frightened child would be to turn around on the spot and leave the house. But this never even crosses her mind; she does not even seem to consider it. She does the very opposite. Instead of fleeing in fright, she comes closer, goes to the bed, and pulls back the curtain.

Her conduct does not strike me as all that amazing. After the wolf's questions and Little Red Riding Hood's exact description, one would have to be very naive or terribly stupid to assume that the grandmother is alone. The little girl is neither naive nor stupid. She may be anxious and irritated—for after all, it is no trivial matter watching one's parents "do it"—but she is more curious than anything else, and she most certainly wished for this situation. Perhaps she even planned it. For how zealously and precisely she described the road to the wolf! If this is so, then the plot is determined not by the big, bad wolf, but by "dear, sweet Little Red Riding Hood." I would consider her capable of it as I would consider all little girls, past, present, and future, capable of similar activities and manipulations. I fear we tend to underestimate our daughters.

Little Red Riding Hood has done it. She now sees what children, even today, almost never see, and she makes some astonishing discoveries. Her grandmother has changed in an almost eerie way and seems totally unfamiliar. Her image is bizarrely mingled with that of the wolf, and, as can be discerned despite the nightcap and nightgown, the grandmother looks quite awful—because of the hairy hand, for instance. It was not necessarily the hand. In fairy tales as in dreams, any organ can be represented by any other. This holds, of course, even for the ears, eyes, and mouth.

In any case, Little Red Riding Hood is fascinated. She is amazed at everything she sees, and she comments on her discoveries. Each of her sentences begins, "Why, Grandmother," which greatly contradicts the possibility that the poor heroine is absolutely paralyzed with fear and terror. Little girls are not frightened all that easily.

"Why, Grandmother," says Little Red Riding Hood in amazement, "what big ears you have!"

She is not asking a question here; nor does she ask any questions further along. One only assumes she is asking questions, because she receives answers. However, her sentences are really statements, surprised statements, exclamations, and I believe that in reality she does not say a single word out loud. She only thinks these comments, for she is witnessing a scene in which adults would never tolerate the presence of a child. One peep out of her and she wouldn't be allowed to witness anything else.

Little Red Riding Hood was most likely not surprised about the organs specified in the fairy tale. Nevertheless, these organs are hardly picked at random. Children have "big ears" when they want to hear something that they are not supposed to hear. And when they find out something about their parents' love life, it is usually by way of their ears. Little Red Riding Hood, too, must have first heard something. Less frequent is the opportunity to have "big eyes" and actually to see this secret instead of just listening to it. However, almost no child will ever manage to be as direct and close a witness of this "primal scene" as the heroine of our fairy tale. She has the possibility and she has the courage to get at the bottom of the most mysterious thing in the world. She does not look away, she does not repress, and she is not ashamed. She pulls the curtain aside and looks, looks very carefully, and all curious children can look over her shoulder, watch with her, listen with her, and even feel with her all the mysterious and secretive things that are going on. Little Red Riding Hood offers all children front-row seats at the primal human scene.

There is no way we could compete. There is no way we could outdo this graphically sensuous scene with its immediate symbols. No amount of technology will help. Compared with fairy tales, all pictures and movies seem shallow and vapid; and no matter how carefully we select our words, they sound sterile. They will never enable us to enlighten any child about the most complicated of human relationships. We cannot even approximately explain feelings to children. We can only meagerly inform them about objective facts. Usually, this may do no harm, but it will not help very much.

Little Red Riding Hood goes one step further. Not only does she watch and describe her many sensual impressions; she wants a lot more—she wants to know precisely what is going on. That is why she gives up her relatively secure (compared with what follows) spectator position and lets herself be drawn into the scene. Of course, this, too, does not happen factually. The little girl receives as few answers as she asks questions. Indeed, she is still on the sidelines, watching. She gets involved in the action only through her mind, her imagination. However, for children, the line between fantasy and reality is a lot blurrier than for adults. They often actually experience what they imagine.

And there is something else that children can do. They can identify with others, especially with their parents, and girls particularly with their mothers.

Little Red Riding Hood does both these things here.

"Why, Grandmother, what big eyes you have," says the little girl.

"The better to see you with," is the answer.

And now the wolf's eyes focus on the child. The child is no longer passive; she joins in and experiences what it is like to be seen by the wolf in this way. Under his gaze, she realizes that these eyes are very different from her grandmother's; they are very big. Even stranger are the large, hirsute hands. "The better to grab you with," is the answer in the Brothers Grimm. In Bechstein: "The better to grab you and hold you with." And finally, in the French version: "The better to embrace you."

There is nothing about such functions of male arms in storybooks. No one tells children anything about this, and even love stories describe the hands of lovers only as caressing. But here, they grab the heroine; they are domineering, possessive, rough, and yet sensuous and tender.

Little Red Riding Hood registers the action. She is not frightened. Perhaps she thinks to herself, "So this is what it's like." Then she comes to the final, albeit highly disconcerting organ. She does not say, "Why, Grandmother," she says, "But Grandmother, what a dreadfully big mouth you have!" Little Red Riding Hood, previously so courageous and self-assured, is knocked slightly off balance by this dreadfully big thing, and her reaction is understandable.

Nevertheless, Little Red Riding Hood still does not run away.

She shows no sign of fear or terror, nor does she let on whether she has seen enough. No, she waits to see what this organ is all about. "The better to eat you with," she hears, and then, according to the original version, the wolf pounces on poor Little Red Riding Hood and devours her.

So this is what happens; but a little girl cannot really understand it—not the words and not what happens next. The *petite mort*, the "little death" (in the French version), that Little Red Riding Hood experiences plunges her into profound darkness; she is at the end of her tether, and she is not equal to the situation that she has evoked. She experiences something that she cannot understand, classify, or digest.

The wolf is in an altogether different state. He, as we learn in Grimm, has "sated his lust," and now he does what so many men, so many husbands, do: he turns over, falls asleep, and snores.

Our heroine has overestimated herself. She has slipped into a situation that she cannot escape unaided.

The moralists can rub their hands and smugly gloat: "That's what she gets. If she had obeyed her mother, nothing would have happened to her." And they may conclude: "Children should keep their noses out of things that do not concern them."

Fine. But if children did not stick their noses into everything, if they were always obedient and well behaved, they would have no experiences of their own; and yet such experiences are the most instructive. And if children did not occasionally test their limits, and occasionally experience failure, they would never get to know themselves or their strength. Besides, such experiments seldom kill them. This is shown by the heroine. She survives the adventure unscathed, for no sooner does she get out of the wolf's belly than she utters a friendly "Good morning" (in Bechstein). It also turns out that she has learned from her experiences. Her mother's words did not do it, but her experience does teach her something: she promptly runs off, gets rocks, and stuffs them into the monster's belly. The wolf, with whom she chatted so amiably and flirted so self-confidently, has now become wicked in her eyes. She has returned to her mother, to her mother's protection and standards, and she is safe once again. The hunter skins the "old sinner." Then all three of them are delighted. The grandmother no longer lies in bed; she is slightly out of breath after her experience with the wolf, which we can understand, but otherwise, she is "fresh and healthy again" (Bechstein), no longer sick and weak. Together, they drink the wine and eat the cake.

So much for that. The world is back in joint and everyone is happy. Little Red Riding Hood had to become well behaved again, and that is good, for she is too young for the wolf and hence indigestible. She still needs her parents and a few more years until she can stop misconstruing sex as "eating." Then, of course, her interest in the wolf and his intentions will no longer be merely academic. Being a big girl, she will know how to deal with him and will very frequently determine the course of events. Many wolves, to be sure, will not notice.

But that's life, for that's what girls are like, little ones and big ones, and we have to live with them. Now, I may not be able to work up as much enthusiasm as Charles Dickens, but I do find Little Red Riding Hood sweet.

The Boy Who Set Out to Learn Fear

The story of a boy who is laughed at by everyone but nevertheless sticks to his goal, who is rejected by his father, chats with corpses, tussles with ghosts, and is ultimately rewarded, finding happiness with a princess.

A FATHER has two sons. The older one is named Matthes, and he is a scaredy-cat (Bechstein). He is timid by nature. He doesn't like to walk past a graveyard in the dark, and he gets goose pimples when ghost stories are told by the fireside at night. However, this is his only failing. Otherwise, he is no fool; he is smart as a whip. He can adjust to anything, makes efforts, and when there is something to be done, he does it well.

The second son, Hans, envies his elder brother, but not for his positive qualities. He is quite indifferent to them. Hans envies him because Matthes can get scared—in contrast to Hans. The younger brother is not bothered by crossing a dark cemetery, and he feels no trace of terror when hearing ghost stories. That is why he wants to learn how to be scared. He says, "It must be a skill that I don't understand at all."

Understandably, Matthes laughs at him and thinks, "Goodness, what a numbskull my brother is. He'll never make anything of himself." The father shares this opinion; he feels that Hans is a hopeless case. And other people think so, too. They believe that the father will have his hands full with Hans.

Hans is considered stupid, unproficient at anything, unable to grasp or learn anything. They say he does everything wrong and is slow on the uptake.

But just as Hans is unable to be scared, so also is he totally indifferent to people's bad opinion of him. Their attitude neither disturbs nor annoys him, for he lives a carefree, innocent, happy-go-lucky life, the way stupid people live. His motto is: "Hans, don't learn too much, otherwise you'll have to do too much."

Who would want such a son?

Matthes is a horse of a different color! He is not only smart as a whip, but also sharp and clever. So what difference does it make that he's scared of the dark? There are many boys who would not want to cross a graveyard at night.

Nevertheless, it is not the well-behaved and popular Matthes who is the hero of this fairy tale. He is only a trivial and peripheral character who is no longer mentioned after the first page. The main role is played by Hans. He serenely overcomes all obstacles, conquers all adversaries, and gets the beautiful princess in the end.

What is so special about him?

Nothing, I would think. Like many fairy-tale heroes, he is a typical child—in this case, a typical boy. Just as many boys are by nature not very industrious and try to make life as pleasant and comfortable for themselves as possible, so, too, Hans is not at all eager to work. Just as many boys are uninterested in what they are supposed to learn and more interested in what they *want* to learn, so, too, Hans is interested in being scared, and that's all.

He is different in only one way: he says what he thinks; he reveals the motto he lives by—and that's usually not done. Such honesty is undesirable, and Hans promptly feels the consequences. He is slandered because of his attitude and put down as naive and stupid. Yet he is anything but this—at least, not stupid. His motto is by no means unintelligent. Hans is practical, useful, and even successful. Whenever the father wants to have something done, he has to let Matthes do it. "Stupid Hans" can sit in his corner and chuckle up his sleeve.

Hans is never scared. Now, this does not mean that boys generally have no fears. They have a number of weak spots in this area, and in some ways they are more timid than girls. However, fear of graveyards is not a typical response for boys. On the contrary, any such timidity is usually outweighed by curiosity and a yen for adventure.

One of the best children's books, Mark Twain's *Adventures of Tom Sawyer*, contains a graveyard scene. The young hero and his friend Huckleberry Finn watch the midnight exhumation of a corpse in the light cast by lanterns. Boys are fascinated by such things, and some may dream of finding buried treasure under dead men's bones in a tomb.

That's what many boys are like.

But, naturally, Matthes is also typical. He is typical of what parents wish their sons to be. Good citizens have raised their children along such lines since the start of the modern age; and as a rule, their efforts have been successful. This parental goal has been supported by society. Whether at school, at church, or in the media, there has been only one type of boy: the Matthes type. Exceptions and deviations were not tolerated—not by fathers and not by teachers and clergymen. Ludwig Richter and other illustrators drew only obedient and well-behaved boys in their readers, children's books, and fairy-tale collections. The accompanying stories and poems about children did not contain any other kind of boy.

Wicked children appear in the famous German book *Struwwelpeter (Slovenly Peter)* by the physician Heinrich Hoffmann. But these children are punished. The ultimate consequences of their deviant behavior are shown as a warning and deterrent. If you play with fire, you'll burn to a crisp. The boy called Suppenkasper winds up in the grave. If a child so much as dreams, then he is punished and nearly drowns. And the thumb-sucker gets both thumbs sliced off, "snip snip." The child screams and the blood spurts.

Wilhelm Busch likewise depicts bad boys in his stories of Max and Moritz. He does delight in telling about their pranks; but in the end, his two boys have to die: they are literally put through a meat grinder, as a dire warning for any possible emulators.

Cooperation in society is the ideal. Thus, lazy, impudent, adventurous, curious, imaginative, dirty, original male children were turned into clean, conformist, well-behaved boys who were able to "adjust to everything." In Matthes, the process has succeeded so perfectly that he identifies with these pedagogical maxims and proclaims, "Just as the twig is bent, the tree's inclined." So he lets himself be bent, and he makes fun of his brother, who won't bend.

Only one genre did not follow the universal trend: the fairy tale. Fairy tales could afford to deviate, for they were viewed as "old wives' tales": they were not taken seriously and hence not supervised. Fairy tales offered (and still offer) alternatives. As this one does.

However, not even the fairy tale lets boyish laziness run riot. The fairy-tale father rouses Hans out of his corner and tells him that he finally has to learn something. He calls him a big, strong lout and names him "Hans Dampf" (literally "Hans Steam," that is, someone who has a finger in every pie). This shows that Hans, obviously no stay-at-home, is enterprising enough, though not in the areas desired by his father (Bechstein). But now he has to learn something in order to make a living later on. Hans decides that he wants to learn how to be scared.

The father can only sigh at this. He assures his son that he will never earn so much as a grain of salt with this ability. Deciding that Hans has to be "licked into shape," he hands him over to his neighbor, the sexton and schoolmaster. The neighbor is convinced that he can quite easily "teach" the boy how to be afraid. "He can learn it splendidly here," the teacher assures the father and takes Hans into his school. This alone, the neighbor believes, can teach the boy fear.

Nor is he all that wrong. Starting school puts an end to a
child's freedom. So much for unlimited playing, so much for
doing only what you feel like. Your mobility is drastically cur-
tailed, and you have to learn things whose purpose you don't
understand. The old saw that generations of parents have been
preaching to generations of children is that school prepares them
for life. This is quite correct, but not comprehensible to a child.
One understands this only when one is grown up. Mainly, school
means confinement for children, deprivation of freedom, coer-
cion. Perceptive educators realize this. Our fairy-tale schoolmaster likewise seems aware of it, or else he very clearly remembers
his own schoolday experiences. In any case, he describes his
school as the "most miserable nest of a house in the entire hamlet,"
and goes on: "I'm scared all day long that it will collapse on me
and kill all the promising brats" (Bechstein).

Can school kill "promising brats"? Indeed it can, for juvenile
spontaneity and originality are not demanded here. Imagination
and independence are suppressed, a child's initiative is not wanted,
adventurousness is not taught, spontaneous interest not heeded.
Children have no natural motivation for the necessary demands,
and rigid rules and regulations obstruct their urge for freedom.
For many, school is indeed a place of fear. This institution most
certainly "kills" all those children who are unsuccessful here and
who are suddenly forced to realize that they may be experts in
climbing trees or building caves but cannot understand reading,
writing, and 'rithmetic.

The Matthes types have an easy time of it. They have already
conformed unconditionally to their fathers' ideal, and they see
that their teachers do not demand anything different. They thus
easily continue their development, and their prospects are not
bad. They will go on conforming, agreeing with everyone else
about what's right, doing what's accepted, believing what the
majority believes, and they will be ashamed of ever being different. These boys will make their way, earn their living, and
attain the necessary recognition. They will have average difficulties and joys in their average lives; nor do they, as a rule,

want anything more. We can let them go their way without further ado.

School is hard on pupils with any originality. No matter what sort of originality they may have, even native wit, the institution of learning fights it. A certain kind of smile can already spell doom for a pupil if a teacher feels provoked by it—and some teachers are easily provoked. Personal opinions are, of course, taboo, and criticism is quite unpopular. However, dreamers and silent types also fail to be accepted; they are forced to wake up and do the only correct and important thing: learn for their future lives. A child with an artistic nature may be highly gifted, but his talents do not impress the school. Such children have to do what's customary—and in the prescribed manner.

The educational institution's viewpoint is that intelligence is conformity. Anyone who does not conform must be stupid; he gets bad marks and is often left back.

For some children, school may be a boon: those with a scholarly aptitude. They are frequently disliked by their fathers, are disparaged at home and often in the street as well, and find a suitable field of activity only in school. They wake up here and develop, gaining strength and self-confidence.

School leaves Hans utterly cold. It doesn't interest or involve him. The ramshackle schoolhouse on the verge of collapse "matters as little to him as to the mayor and the honorable community" (Bechstein). And needless to say, he does not learn how to be scared here.

So the sexton thinks of "some other device"; this, he feels, cannot fail to teach Hans how to be scared. He wakes him at midnight, tells him to get up, climb to the church spire, and ring the bell. The sexton then secretly goes on ahead, drapes himself in a white sheet, stations himself on the stairway opposite the louver window, and starts moaning terribly when Hans reaches for the bell rope.

Evidently, the sexton doesn't know boys. Old church towers are terribly attractive to them, but normally have the disadvantage of being not only off limits but also locked up. Now Hans can actually enter the tower quite officially, ring the bell in the middle of the night, and wake up the whole village with impunity. There's nothing terrifying about this; it's fun. And there's an additional bonus: Hans is pinch-hitting for the sexton, and all boys love to play adult parts. Hans now plays the sexton, that is, the master of the house. An unauthorized person appears, and the boy challenges him: "Who are you?" he cries. "What do you want?" The figure keeps silent. Hans repeats his question in a "louder voice" and advises the intruder, "Answer me or get out of here. You have no business being here at night."

Thus, Hans does not hastily resort to unconsidered actions; he does not exceed his authority. He does not play his part badly.

The sexton remains "rigid and immobile," in order to make the boy believe that he is a ghost. But this thought never crosses the boy's mind; he associates the intruder with something quite different: "Don't you have a mouth, snowman?" he asks him and then threatens to toss him down the stairs if he doesn't answer.

By now at the very latest, the sexton should realize that his plan has gone awry. But no, he keeps trying, doesn't let out a peep, and remains standing as if he were "made of stone." He makes a further mistake; he thinks, "He doesn't really mean it." Here, too, he deceives himself about the mentality of boys. Often, unlike their parents, they follow through on things and stick to their word.

Hans's threats are not idle; nevertheless, he challenges the apparition once again. (He cannot really be reproached for anything.) It is only upon seeing that his challenge is useless that he charges the figure and throws him down the stairs. The figure remains lying in the corner. Hans then performs his assigned task and "swings the bell rope with a vengeance" (Bechstein).

The sexton has not performed his task. Yet he was so sure of himself! He could be sure of himself, for people normally respect the institutions he represents. They knuckle under in school, and they fear God and his church. The building itself makes this hierarchy clear: it looms high above people's houses, and its bells are louder than anything else.

But Hans is impressed by neither the school nor the church tower. Nor does he look up to the sexton; on the contrary, he has identified with him and imitated him. The sexton may have taken this behavior into account, for he has not approached the boy personally, on an official or human level, but as an anonymous entity. That's how he appears to him in the dead of night, at a significant hour and in a lofty place. Most people would have been impressed by the sexton's appearance. They would have taken this eerie figure for a ghost, and what with his appearing in the tower of the house of God, they would not have mistaken him for the devil.

This is what the sexton wants. His apparition, he hopes, should represent the anonymous authority of the powers that he normally serves. He demonstrates their strength. He thus wants to force Hans to his knees and scare him.

Hans is not scared. The unknown does not scare him. He only wants to know who it is and what it is. But he receives no answer, not even to his further questions.

The old, venerable social institutions do not answer any questions. They have already supplied all the answers, proclaiming them to mankind. As written and unwritten laws, as dogmas and postulates of faith, they stand rigid and immobile, as though carved in stone. The small, insignificant person has to adjust accordingly, obey, believe, and go along with the demands and instructions. He must ask no questions, for social norms are not open to question or discussion, even though they may be as "worn, rotten, narrow, and filled with centuries-old dust" as the steps of the village church or as rickety and ramshackle as the old schoolhouse (Bechstein).

But our hero cannot realize this as yet; he cannot grasp these social values. He responds in his own way: with naiveté and physical action. Naturally, his action does not solve the problem, and that is why he does not throw the inadequate representative of an antiquated principle from his rotten pedestal; he merely tosses the poor sexton down the stairs.

The sexton's fate, I believe, is not so undeserved. After all, he took his task too easily and performed it poorly, for he did not even attempt to keep his promise and teach the boy anything. All he could come up with was the idea of terrifying him and offering him a dubious demonstration of power.

If institutions have to keep silent when asked curious questions by small boys, the sexton could at least have answered as a human being. He could have dropped his silly disguise, which, as he noticed, was futile, and he could have had an intimate conversation with Hans in the dark tower. He did not do so; he did not go that far. Like the father, he leaves the boy alone with his problems, fails to help him, explains nothing to him, devotes no time to him, shows no understanding for him.

He acts like many fathers and educators, who do nothing more than teach children the necessary norms by means of fear and terror, stuffing them full of lifeless knowledge.

Some boys put up with this, others do not; and a lot more than we think have their own ideas and behave in their own fashion. But they do not show us this, do not talk about it, for they know how we will react: just like the father and the sexton. Who would expose himself voluntarily to such treatment? We learn from Hans what he is thinking; he gives voice to his thoughts and shows his feelings. Thus, even after throwing the "ghost" down the stairs, he is not aware of having done anything wrong; he rings the bell "as if nothing had happened," and he "climbs down the stairs cheerfully." He does not bother about the yammering "ghost"; he lets him lie. And when he finds out that it was the sexton whom he knocked down the stairs, his only response, terse and unimpressed, is "Really!" (Bechstein).

That's what boys are like. Many have such a naive, consistent, but also rigorous morality. Yet we do not let them be with their morality. By means of our educational techniques, we make them conform to our standards. Most boys do this, more or less outwardly. But any boy who openly refuses, resists, digs in his heels, will get into serious trouble, as our fairy-tale hero now does.

He gives the sexton's wife a sober and truthful account of what happened up in the tower. In the Bechstein version, he says, "A white nincompoop was standing on the stairs. He wouldn't answer my questions, so I shoved him down the steps. He's still lying there and moaning." In Grimm, he is somewhat more courteous: "Just go over and see whether it's him. I'm sorry." But in neither version does he care to answer for what he has done; he feels no responsibility for the consequences of his action. Hence, it never occurs to him to offer to help the sexton's wife. He only sends her over.

For her, the decisive issue is the consequence of Hans's action. Her husband is injured, the boy did it; hence it is his fault, and hence he is bad. She yells at Hans and grabs the keys from him. This may not be fair to the boy, but it is understandable. She calls him a good-for-nothing and then runs, screaming, to Hans's father and tells him what a horrible thing his son has done.

We can pause briefly here and wonder how the father will now react. He certainly has a wealth of possibilities. Yet he is obviously unaware of this choice, and he apparently does not stop to consider what he should do. In any event, he does not hold back for an instant; he promptly becomes "totally wild," screams, calls Hans a "ne'er-do-well," shoves money into his hand, and says, "Get out! Start moving!" (Bechstein). And then adds: "You can get hanged wherever you like." In the Grimm version, he says that Hans's pranks are godless and must have been inspired by the Evil One.

Hans defends himself sensibly and factually. After all, he had good reasons. But they are useless.

"Ah," says the father, "I get nothing but misery from you. Get out of my sight. I never want to see you again."

I fear that with his "Ah!" the father is expressing pity for himself and not his son. He wants nothing more to do with his offspring; he is ashamed of him and disowns him. "Go out into the wide world," he tells Hans, "and never tell anyone where you come from or who your father is."

Hans gets to know the realities of life here. He learns that when a child is unimpressed by the world of grownups and their institutions, he will be punished like a criminal, and, if he proves superior to even one of their representatives, he will be ruthlessly expelled. In such a case, even parental solidarity with children ends. For the father, his neighbors and his standing in the community are more important than his son. He disowns his own son and drives him out.

Nor is there much justice in the world, as Hans realizes. The sexton's wife considers him a scoundrel who has played a rotten trick on her husband, and she curses the boy. It never crosses her mind that it was the sexton who tried to hoodwink Hans and that the boy was simply reacting and defending himself. Hans also sees now that there are important personages in this society who stand way above most grownups. One has to know and respect them. Woe to you if you mistake them for "snowmen" and make fools of them. Anyone who does so will be considered godless, in league with the evil powers, and destined for the gallows.

Hans registers this—and everything else—calmly. None of it bothers him, and he does not feel obligated to behave accordingly. He remains a happy-go-lucky ignoramus.

Hans has not learned to be scared either at home with his parents, at school, or in church. So he turns elsewhere, to new things and people, outside his family and the confining village. He goes out on the "great highway." He has not given up on his goal. "If only I were scared!" he says to himself. His wish is overheard by a man, who behaves quite differently from what Hans is accustomed to. The man does not poke fun at him, does not deride him; he deals with him quite matter-of-factly. He shows him a gallows with seven corpses and advises him to spend a night there. The man is friendly and calls Hans a good buddy (Bechstein). Hans promises to give him his fifty gold pieces if he learns how to be scared in this way.

This frequently happens to boys. In the outside world, they are recognized; but at home, they are not taken seriously. All too often, a family inhibits a child's development; it is opposed to letting a little boy become a big boy. This is not purely negative, for the boy must overcome their opposition, which can help him grow. Such is the case with Hans. He has managed to outgrow the confines of parental attachment, and the reward for this necessary developmental step is money. If a man has money, we are told, he needn't be scared. Hans is capable of dealing with a strange man. He has sufficient self-confidence and self-assurance.

Following the man's advice, he settles under the gallows and starts a fire. The fire illuminates the seven "shaking" corpses above him as the raw night wind knocks them to and fro. Hans by no means averts his head; he looks carefully at the bodies and ascertains that these are poor devils hanging up there. "You're so cold that you're clattering and rattling," he says and climbs up the gibbet ladder, unties the hanged men, and places them around his fire to warm them. He observes them carefully and finds that they look absolutely wretched, "green, yellow, and lamentable, shiny blue, awful." They don't move, don't stir; instead they let their rags and tatters catch fire. This angers Hans. He takes the "dead corpses" and hangs them up again, "one after the other" (Bechstein). Then he wraps himself up in his coat, stetches out cozily, and falls asleep.

So far, he hasn't been scared. He is too stupid or, more precisely, too young. It is not to his credit that he is unimpressed; his age is the reason. Death means nothing to him as yet; he does not yet have to live with the thought that every minute of his life brings him closer to the grave. He is in a far better position than we. We know about death, we fear it, and when we encounter death, we are deeply affected. Its alien quality frightens us profoundly, as does its irrevocable silence. Being alone with a dead man, who no longer reacts, who will never react again, who is gone from us, a human being and yet no human being— all this makes us feel empty and lonely. Man, the social creature, cannot endure such things. He is dependent on feedback from others, on exchange. Death denies him these things.

Our hero is totally unconcerned about this reality. He alters it with the help of his imagination and speaks cheerfully to the discolored corpses. Only a boy can have this kind of reaction.

Children do not know death. When they learn that someone

has died, they may ask, "When will he come back?" Being dead has initially no other meaning for them than being away. Death becomes terrifying and incomprehensible only through the reactions of adults. When Father or Mother mourns, weeps, shows despair, loses mental stability, then children grow confused and react with fear. We then assume that they, too, feel grief. But as a rule, this is not the case. One can readily take children to funerals. So long as the parents are present and are able to give them attention, the ceremony will frighten them as little as the gallows hill frightens Hans. Children do not have our associations. They do not connect a coffin, flowers, organ music, and the hole in the ground with their dead grandma.

And why should they?

Much later, when they no longer—never again—find Grandmother in the familiar surroundings, they may realize that there is something more definitive than absence. These are the times that sadden them, not the burial ceremony. Boys like Hans may have technical thoughts at a funeral—they may wonder what will happen if a rope breaks while the coffin is being lowered.

That's what boys are like.

But they don't stay that way. They learn more, and soon they know how to act in the presence of death. This knowledge is not imparted by instruction; no one teaches or explains it to them. They merely copy our behavior. They are scared because we are scared; they circle around an eerie gallows because we circle around it. They are sad because we are sad, and they fear death because everyone fears it. They take over our feelings.

This is how children learn. They do so automatically and without reflection. Without giving it a second thought, they will exhibit grief when a relative dies, even if it's an aunt that no one liked or a rich uncle. They'll be delighted when a nasty enemy dies, even if he was a good person. They will not mourn when a criminal is executed. They will not pity a murderer, but they will glorify a warrior because he killed lots of enemies. As soldiers, they will cheerfully kill and die for the fatherland, for a good cause, or whatever.

Through instruction, they learn the Fifth Commandment: Thou shalt not kill. But when push comes to shove, it won't help. Learning by imitation is more effective.

Hans is the hero of this story because he refuses to learn in this way. He does not adopt unthinkingly the thoughts and feelings of his father and the sexton, the things that other people view as correct or proper. Hans remains free of these influences. This makes him an interesting construction, a 200-proof boy, as it were, with no patina of civilization, but also with no cultural refinement.

If he wanted to know something about death, he would ask why we cry for the rich uncle from whom we inherit so much money, or for the aunt who was so obnoxious. He would want to know why a war hero is no murderer, even though he deliberately kills people, and whether it's really true that when we die we go to heaven, a place from which no one has ever come back.

Little boys ask such questions. But normally, they ask only once, for they easily perceive by our reactions how unsuitable and uncomfortable we find these questions, and so they hold back their curiosity. They conform. They do so at the cost of their undistorted naturalness. We harm them when we wave off their questions as stupid. Their questions are not stupid; they have a realistic, albeit impious, logic. We ought to answer them, truthfully and without hypocrisy. If we take our children's concerns seriously, we strengthen their self-confidence and increase their self-assurance.

Our hero finds no sympathy for his problem and receives no answers to his questions. So he goes forth in quest of adventures, in order to gather his own experiences. The night on the gallows tree has afforded him little insight. However, he can keep his fifty gold pieces, and the man goes off empty-handed. The man is surprised; he has never run into anyone like this, and he feels that Hans will never learn how to be scared.

But Hans wants to learn it, and he has to learn it. This boy must be scared of something; he must eventually be impressed, touched, deeply moved, otherwise he will remain trapped in his childhood realism, never to mature, never to grow up, never to become a man. Perhaps he senses this. In any case, he murmurs to himself, "Ah, if only I could be scared!"

He is overheard by a drayman, who then tells him his version of being scared (Bechstein). He gets scared in the tavern, because the innkeeper presents such "hair-raising" bills. He has always felt chills up and down his spine upon getting them. If Hans has money and would like to drop in at the tavern, he will learn how to be scared, says the drayman.

"Let's see!" says Hans. He seems unconvinced that this will lead him to his goal. Nevertheless, he thanks the drayman and enters the tavern. When the innkeeper asks him what he would like, he says, "I would like to learn how to be scared." And he goes on, "People on the highway say that I can easily learn it here. You make such scary bills and wield such scary chalk!" This should get a good laugh from the customers. The innkeeper is less enthusiastic and thinks, "I'll teach you a thing or two—you'll be scared, all right!" Out loud, he amiably informs Hans that he has been "told falsehoods" and that he, the innkeeper, never treats customers the way "some lying fool" would have Hans believe.

The hero is anything but naive in this situation. He knows his way, finds the right tone, and boldly makes fun of the innkeeper. His fifty gold pieces are in no danger of changing hands.

The innkeeper recommends an enchanted castle for teaching Hans how to be scared. Anyone who frees the castle of its poltergeists will be richly rewarded and get to marry the king's daughter—needless to say, only if he escapes with his life. "And what if I don't escape with my life, what then?" asks Hans.

Here he asks this question. But the innkeeper laughs in his face. "I can tell you've got a cunning head on your shoulders," says the innkeeper. "You would certainly have invented gunpowder if it hadn't been invented already!"

Hans is shown that one does not ask such questions. Gunpowder has already been invented. The questions have been answered once and for all by the appropriate institutions, and the answers are well known. But adolescents nevertheless ask them.

Hans wants to go to the castle. He goes "up there"—he leaves the lowland. He leaves behind the man from the highway, who is afraid of (harmless) corpses; the drayman, who cannot determine his own behavior, who is weak and lets himself be cheated out of money; the innkeeper, who profits from the weakness of his fellow men and is too cowardly to go to the castle himself, win the princess, and become rich.

None of these people can impress Hans, any more than his father, the school, or the sexton can. Boys are not only unsentimental realists, they are also purists and moralists. Using these standards, they measure us, discern our failings and foibles, our banality, and turn away from us in disappointment. They consider themselves better, more decent, more moral, more righteous, and even more tolerant. They never doubt any of this at all.

Consistent with this assessment, Hans goes up. From up there, he can look down on us, which will seem suitable to him. But he also has to bear the consequences for this voluntary isolation, for he will be lonely and solitary. He is ready for this and accepts the conditions.

He goes to the king. He acknowledges him and says with extreme politeness (something often lacking at his age), "If I may, I would like to spend three nights in the enchanted castle" (Grimm). The king looks at him, likes him on the spot, amiably calls him "son" (Bechstein), and allows him to take three things along to the castle, although they must be lifeless objects.

The king is also a father, but of a very different sort from Hans's father. He takes Hans seriously and does not try to talk him out of his goal. He does not claim that Hans is too young, too stupid, too immature, or in any way unfit. The king does not moralize or lament. He respects Hans's wish and supports him with useful things. He acts like a sensible, understanding friend. A model father!

He has only one shortcoming. He is not real; fathers like him do not exist. He is an ideal, a product of Hans's wishful thinking.

This is how he pictures a father, and he measures fathers by this image. Hans is not the only boy in the world to nurture such an image. More or less all adolescent sons expect the king's conduct from their fathers. Hence, it is not surprising that conflicts emerge. Many people call this state of conflict the generation gap. Their view is only partially accurate. These conflicts arise because our sons demand too much. We cannot live up to their notions. It is impossible for us to be that tolerant, generous, magnanimous, and goodness knows what else. This incapacity makes the conflicts inevitable. They are programmed into the development of children. The well-known gap is necessary so that our children may become independent and self-sufficient. This development is much easier if they can find us bad: negative, old-fashioned, authoritarian, narrow-minded, unsympathetic. This makes it possible for them to reject us. They can break their attachment to us and go their own way. This is precisely what they now have to do.

Perhaps we can endure our nerve-wracking conflicts more easily if we understand these dynamics. The conflicts are practically unavoidable. Our growing children need them. Nor would we help our children by giving in to them. They need our resistance. Although they claim the opposite, we would lose their respect if we denied our own positions for their sake (in order to more closely resemble their ideal image). They would consider us weak, as Hans does the drayman.

Hans has broken away; he has become able and also willing to try his luck alone, to have adventures on his own and gather experiences. This is not so easy, and anyone attempting it must reckon with the kind of setting described in our fairy tale: a haunted castle deserted by all living things and standing at a lonesome height.

Hans is now there, in a room. He has started a bright fire in the huge fireplace, for one of the three lifeless things he chose was material for the fire. He also asked for a lathe and a carver's bench. The king had these objects brought into the castle during the day.

Now the night is coming, and we will have to see whether the boy is up to the ordeals that life holds for him—and all boys of his age. No one can help him with the tasks and problems awaiting him. No one is here to offer him support or comfort. He has to cope with everything alone.

This prospect does not frighten him. He sits on his lathe, warms himself at the fire, and repeats his old wish: "Ah, if only I were scared." And he does not believe that he will learn how to be scared here.

We may often complain about the high-handed and arrogant ways of our adolescents. But they have to be overbearing and full of themselves; otherwise they would lose their nerve and run back to Mom and Dad and the safe nest. Who, aside from a boy of this age, would have the courage to look forward with such composure to the highly dangerous events in the castle? Frankly, I would have left the castle by now. And quite rightly, as the next few events show. For suddenly, at midnight, there is a scream from a corner: "Oh, meow! We're freezing!" And two big black cats stare at Hans with eyes of "green fire" (Bechstein).

The boy really has no other possibility than to be tremendously frightened. He could learn how to be scared, and the matter would be done with.

But our hero does not react in this way. On the contrary, he even invites the ugly creatures to join him by the fireside—and he is neither intimidated nor polite. Oh no. "You fools," he shouts, "why are you screeching? If you're freezing, then come, sit down by the fire and warm yourselves."

He does exactly the right thing. This is the only way that he can deal with the cats. He needs the qualities that we set so little store by. He has to act arrogant and insolent, otherwise he'd be a goner.

Nevertheless, he is still far from winning the first round, for now the two cats take huge leaps. One lands to his left, the other to his right, and they look at him "wildly with their fiery eyes" (Grimm).

Hans is undaunted; he waits. "We're bored," the animals lament. They want to play cards with Hans, and, at his request, they produce a deck (Bechstein). But Hans doesn't like the terrible claws on their black paws. "Show me your paws," he demands. The creatures stretch out their claws.

The conflict has begun. The hero must not only not put up passively with the eerie things that happen to him, he has to resist actively. He is as unimpressed as ever in his conduct. "Oh!" he says. "What long nails you have. Wait, I'll have to clip them first." Bechstein has him say, "Excuse me, but your mother has not cut your nails for a long time. You should be ashamed of yourselves. Come, I'll file them for you."

In both versions, he grabs the animals and traps their paws in the lathe. Needless to say, they put up a fight and try to sink their fangs into him. "Now that I've seen your fingers," he says, "I don't feel like playing cards." He kills them and throws them out into the moat.

That's how it happens, very simply. He does not stop to think, he does not weigh any ifs, ands, or buts, he does not consult his conscience. He acts, and without scruples. If he had any, and if he weren't so ruthless, he would be doomed.

We complain about this severity of our young people. Some adults accuse them of being coarse and brutal. These qualities are certainly bad and also useless for later life. However, this transitional phase is not later life; adolescents now need all their strength for coping with the many challenges they encounter. Hans, too, needs all his strength, for things get worse for him. A mob of horribly screeching black cats and dogs emerge from every corner. They jump into his fire, pull it apart, and try to extinguish it. For a while, Hans watches them calmly. But when it gets too much for him, he grabs his carving knife and shouts, "Get out of here, you riffraff!" and he starts beating them. Some of them flee, the others he kills and tosses outside.

He thus wins the first round.

The cats are Hans's peers; more precisely, they display conduct typical of male peers, namely their preference for joining into negative groups. These groups have always existed; but they have, understandably, never been popular. They like to charge through streets, rowdy and noisy, shrieking horribly. And they dislike all middle-class virtues, including cleanliness. Black paws and long nails are expressions of their notion of personal freedom. Their games are no longer childhood games. They've broken with their parents, rejecting their influence. They think of themselves as very strong and manly. But they are neither. In reality, these poor devils feel quite alone, even lonely and abandoned. "Ooh, we're freezing!" they yammer in the fairy tale. A telling image. You see, they have not outgrown their parents. They can't do without them. So they take refuge in a group. Here, they at least find a little warmth, even recognition, support, and, last but not least, understanding.

We always see these groups only from the outside and experience only their aggressiveness. But the members act differently toward one another. Aside from internal power struggles, they stick together and help each other. In the group, they feel strong. They need this sense of strength, for alone they are weak and insecure; nor do they feel all that comfortable in their role. This is one reason why they recruit more members; the larger the crowd, the smaller the doubt. Hence, they missionize, and their proselytizing is not exactly delicate. Threats and intimidation are established methods: the two cats take a powerful leap, and land next to Hans. Flanking him and wildly rolling their eyes, they leave him little chance of not joining in.

The scene shows how attractive such groups may seem. Yet those who become members of such a group gain nothing. They exchange one dependency for another. The group provides only a poor surrogate for domestic attachments. The members lose their individuality, become only a part of the whole, and are forced uncompromisingly to do what the others do. Our fairy tale does not even grant these juveniles a human status; it depicts them as animals.

Hans is not scared of them, for they are part of his world and familiar to him. He watches their carryings-on calmly. He needs his defensive energy when they get too close for comfort, violently encroaching on his space. Now he has to defend himself. Everyone knows how difficult that is.

Adolescent severity is very useful in resisting the pressure and influence of these forces. Overly well-behaved boys are a lot worse off in these situations. A boy who has never gone against his parents and has always conformed is in danger of acting similarly here. Matthes wouldn't stand a chance.

Of course, insolence and arrogance alone will save no one. Other powers and faculties are needed here. Hans has them. He is pursuing a goal and he knows what he wants. He is even ready to spend his good money for knowledge and experience. He does not suffer from boredom, he knows how to use the lathe and the carver's bench, and he has not broken with everything his parents taught him. He was polite to his father, even when his father was unfair and unsympathetic. Nevertheless, Hans can put up a resistance and say no. And he can do something that few adolescents can do: he can be alone.

Hans also knows how to deal with the cats. He does not compromise himself by being overfriendly, nor does he provoke a conflict on the spot. He invites them to warm up at his fire.

He thus shows his solution to the problem and recommends the solution to others. He has not looked to others to replace the lost warmth of the nest; he has built his own fire. In this way, he has obtained the warmth he needs and does not have to freeze.

The cats want to play cards, but not 500 Rummy—they want to play a game of chance, *Pochen* (poker), once forbidden and outlawed, especially for minors. The deck of cards that they pull out of their pockets used to be seen as the devil's prayer book.

Hans is certainly no model boy, and he is quite familiar with this game. He is not enthusiastic, but he is nevertheless willing to play poker with them. But the moment he sees their black paws and long nails, he changes his mind.

Hans has something else, of which his fellow players haven't the foggiest notion: he has pride. He does not play with just anyone. And something else is revealed: since he does not reject all the rules, customs, and mores of his parents' home, he feels that nails have to be cut, and that someone who doesn't cut his nails ought to be ashamed. Indeed, he says so.

Hans does not need to emphasize his independence by flaunting external things. Lack of grooming does not make a boy virile, and long nails (or hair) do not make him free. That's as true today as it was back then.

Hans rejects the cats' company. He prefers not to join in, not to participate in the prohibited game. His is a moral decision. He is risking a conflict. This makes his decision even weightier.

The other group, which is merely noisy, rowdy, and destructive, does not impress him either. He separates himself from them; his knife symbolizes his decision. He thus does not really kill them. The cats jump out the window and will probably roam elsewhere.

Hans has no chance to rest on his laurels. This phase of development is extraordinarily dynamic. One problem crops up after another. Hans returns to the fire and finds another visitor. A dog is sitting there with bared teeth and a fiery tongue hanging "out of his throat, the length of an arm" (Bechstein).

I don't want to beat about the bush in regard to a topic that is still embarrassing today, still controversial, and still hushed up: the thing that is so hideously bared at our hero is sexuality, the sex drive, and the thing that hangs down the length of an arm from the huge animal is quite unequivocally a phallic symbol, the stiff penis. Hans has an erection, he is in a stage of sexual excitement. This is typical of his age; every boy gets erections, and most boys get them very often.

The eruption of sexual energy into Hans's life, at a time when he is under terrible psychological stress, is very accurately described as a dog. Consistent with this anything but simple or trivial problem, this creature is neither a lapdog nor a noble animal, and anything but attractive. And equally unattractive are the natural forces, which are brutal during adolescence.

One can sympathize with the hero for his dislike of this new phenomenon. But there it looms, a challenge, and he has to deal with it. All adolescent males have to deal with it, and theirs is no easy task, for they have to face this problem all by themselves. No one helps them, no one advises them, and almost no one has any insight into their trials and tribulations. Society holds its tongue. Despite all the enlightenment and the much-touted sexual liberation, most people still don't talk about sex.

This would not be so bad if the silence were neutral. But it is not neutral. Despite the universal (embarrassed) silence, everyone knows what people in our society think about this matter. Even the adolescent who is dealing with sexual problems knows. He knows quite well that he is supposed to ignore this dog; he is supposed to keep it at bay, remain strong, turn away, and follow his path.

If he does not succeed, if he fails to resist the drive, if he weakens, then he will do what ninety percent of all young people do. Our fairy-tale hero is no exception. He does not hesitate, does not reflect for long, does not consider ignoring the dog for even an instant. For him, such an attempt is no doubt unrealistic. Hans acts, smashing the carving knife "through the dog's teeth and down his maw."

It may be unconvincing to claim that this is an image for adolescent masturbation, for Hans's action has little pleasure or enjoyment; there is nothing sensual about it and there is not a trace of fun. But that's the way it is: an adolescent's satisfaction of his sexual drive is not much fun. He acts quickly and vehemently; it usually lasts no more than a minute and is not very pleasurable for most boys. This is confirmed unequivocally by the words—often forgotten in adulthood—that adolescent boys have been using for generations. None of these words is cheerful or expresses sex or pleasure. Boys say they are beating off, jerking off, beating the meat.

These terms could have fathered the image chosen by the fairy tale, for Hans does something very similar: he knocks off the fiery tongue. The tongue falls down and is no longer fiery. Hans acts quickly and vehemently and is then at peace. This was the purpose of his action.

Hans and most of his fellow adolescents do not strive for pleasure when masturbating. They want to calm down again after being afflicted by their powerful drives; they want to get rid of their nervous tension.

Indeed, the sexual pressure during this developmental phase is greater than at any other time, nor does the high point of sexual activity come during adulthood as many people (understandably) believe. It occurs at the age of sixteen and seventeen. This has been corroborated by all research.

Hans has reached his goal, for, as we are told, "The head departed from the lower body." This may mean that his head is free again, that he can think clearly again, and the tension coming from the lower part has stopped, vanished, like the large, panting dog, which is suddenly gone. Hans thus is calm again, but the dog will return, perhaps daily, certainly several times a week, and then this scene will be repeated. Hans will chop off the long, fiery tongue over and over, but never definitively free himself of the pressure.

Given Western upbringing, Western belief and superstition, our hero has reacted quite well to the challenge posed by the dog; he has at least passed this test, too. As satisfied as he can be under the given circumstances, he goes to bed.

But he has not even fallen asleep when the bed moves "as if drawn by six horses." It drives through the entire castle, upstairs and down, through rooms and halls. Hans enjoys the ride. "Now I see what it's like when the grand lords go driving," he says, and then adds, "Just keep going." The bed does so.

It all sounds very fantastic and improbable, and yet everyone is familiar with this process, which frequently occurs before we drift off. On the borderline between sleeping and waking, when the conscious restraints no longer operate, we begin to dream. Abandoning the here and now, we can play any role and make any wish come true.

Hans does so, and his action is understandable. After all, he has been harshly badgered by physical and mental realities. Our hero builds himself a castle in the air, in the truest sense of the word, and comfortably drives around in it. He feels the way many boys enjoy feeling: like a grand lord, and he loves it. Our boys don't need to fall asleep in order to have such dreams. They are not dependent on the withdrawal of conscious restraints, for they are not yet inhibited about fantasizing. They build themselves cloud castles in any situation, especially during boring hours at school. You can tell by their absent gaze. We may not know what is going on inside them, but we may be fairly certain that their wool-gathering focuses on a strong, invincible hero who can cope with any situation. This hero is the dreamer himself.

Some people, I believe, have managed to salvage their childhood fantasies in their adult lives and written them down. Books and comics with such omnipotent heroes are extremely popular among children. Tarzan is such a classical figure. Batman and Superman, and perhaps Asterix and his powerful friend Obelix, are his modern successors. Many fairy-tale heroes belong in this category, including our Hans.

Such daydreams are useful and positive, and children ought to feel like a "strong man" or "grand lord" occasionally. After all he has gone through, Hans's dreams help him to sleep soundly. "He fell asleep and slept like a log," says Bechstein.

In Grimm, the bed capsizes at the end of its tour and dumps the hero out. This plunges him back into reality. It doesn't bother him; he lies down by the fire and sleeps until daybreak.

In the morning, the king arrives—Hans's dream father, as we should recall here. He looks at the boy on the floor and assumes that he is dead. The king says, "Too bad about this handsome man."

Hans must be delighted, for real fathers do not give such compliments. Good looks, they feel, are (only) for the female sex, and they teach their sons that men should be above such things. However, men are *not* above such things. And we can observe a lot of boys who love to gaze and gaze at themselves in the mirror, grooming their hair, worrying about skin imperfections, and wondering whether they are good-looking, especially in a manly way. Their fathers mostly steal secret glances in mirrors in order to admire themselves. Women, defamed as vain, do not admire themselves in mirrors. They stand in front of a mirror and make themselves beautiful, in order to be admired.

In any case, vanity is no female domain. It is conspicuous in all young people. Their looks are as important to boys as to girls. We should know this, tolerate it, and not put it down.

The king rejoices upon noticing that Hans is still alive, and he envies him for his sound sleep. "If I could sleep that soundly!" he sighs (Bechstein).

Needless to say, Hans is glad to hear this remark. An ideal father, to whom one is nevertheless superior in certain ways— that is the dream of many boys.

When the king asks how he has fared, Hans replies, "Quite well." That's all. He says nothing even to the sympathetic ideal father. He is no longer naively communicative; he no longer bursts out with his nocturnal experiences, as he might have done very recently. The boy has definitely learned a thing or two. He places a necessary distance between himself and others. Hans has become more mature. This is a positive development; it is an important and necessary step toward independence.

However, many parents have a different attitude toward such conduct. They complain about the sudden taciturnity of their sons; they lament that they can't get anything out of them, that their children no longer confide in them, although they could certainly tell them anything, talk to them about anything.

I am afraid these parents overrate themselves. As a rule, they already have a hard time understanding their adolescents' taste. They usually cannot go along with them in regard to their clothing and hair, their preferences in music and literature, or their politics. Presumably, their children's wishes, fantasies, and daydreams would be totally alien to the parents.

But what if the sons were gullible enough (and most of them no longer are) to tell their parents about their experiences with the "cats," about their manners and mores, the forbidden games for money—or the things that would correspond to them now: vandalism, drinking, drug habits? Would parents care to hear about such things? Would they be understanding?

And what kind of grimaces would parents make upon hearing their boys speak forthrightly about their sexual practices, perhaps even in their own vocabulary? Parents might learn that their children's sexual activity is greater than their own.

I fear that mothers and fathers would learn how to be scared, and yet these are only the results of Hans's first night.

Our hero has done what many of his peers do: he has broken the childhood attachment to his parents. In the subsequent transitional phase, parents often really have a hard time, because many sons practically refuse to talk to them. They turn away from their parents. They are no longer interested in their fathers, mothers, or the rest of the family and its concerns. It is almost unbelievable how consistent and radical children can be during this period. There is little one can do about it, and we may be happy if we manage to keep up some sort of dialogue.

Indeed, our boys have other fish to fry now, and they really don't need us. They have learned what they could from us, they are no longer interested in those things, and they turn to something new.

Hans shows this. He has almost forgotten his parents; and at the beginning of the second night, he is at his fire again, alone and on his own. He does not feel lonely and does not suffer, for this is precisely the situation he has wished for. He eagerly waits for new and different experiences. He would like to experience things that he couldn't experience as a child at home and in school, and he wonders whether these new experiences will affect him, tell him anything, appeal to him, or move him. This is what he is waiting for, this is what he is striving for. He wants to be scared, once and for all.

And every effort is made in the castle to teach him this lesson.

For starters, the chimney rattles and shakes, as if the whole structure were about to come down. Next, a man, screaming loudly, comes down the chimney and falls at Hans's feet. But it is only half a man.

Our hero is unimpressed. "Well?" he asks. "What's this all about?" And he demands the second half. "One and a half men," he states, "are no company" (Bechstein).

The boy is still wet behind the ears, but he thinks of himself as a man, and he wants to have a "complete man" for company. Modesty is not characteristic of this age.

Nevertheless, Hans is not all that wrong by his lights, for the half-men, the adolescents, have already been taken care of in the guise of the rowdy dogs and cats. Hans overcame them during the first night. Thus, he now deserves to have a "complete man," and indeed he gets one.

More din, noise, and howling; then the second half falls down. Hans blows on the fire to welcome it. When he looks around, the two halves have already fused, becoming one man; not a handsome man, however, but a hideous one. The man sits on the bench and tries to usurp Hans's seat.

So this is what manhood—so hotly desired by so many boys— looks like! Many boys are terrified by such a massive eruption into their secure mental structure, and they are scared. This stands to reason, for they are truly in a bad state. The new thing is ugly, gross, and brutal, and it takes over in a disagreeable way. The past, on the other hand, collapses; nothing remains of it.

First the boy's voice breaks, and then the entire childhood existence crumbles, after years of being built up and becoming a harmonious whole in puberty. The "completed child" has both feet in life; he is secure and self-confident. He has natural and evident charm, such as one has only during this period. His physical and mental capacity is untroubled and unimpaired. He moves with all his harmony, and possesses a naive immediacy that no adult possesses. And a child can also be truly merry and carefree.

But now childhood is over. The boy gets a beard and pimples. His body becomes disharmonious; his movements are awkward. The boy has no understanding for others; his conduct is unendurable.

This development is demonstrated by Hans. "Move!" he shouts. "That's my seat! Get going or I'll slice you in half with my carving knife!" (Bechstein).

The boy is right. He won't be pushed around. He refuses to be chained by the new phase. Nothing that's offered to him is accepted uncritically. He thereby maintains his own point of view, remains capable of acting as an individual, and thus stays in control of his own mind. However greatly he may wish for manliness, he does not identify with it. If he did identify with it, he would lose all sense of proportion, become unbearably arrogant and presumptuous, and be totally unrealistic in overestimating himself.

This is the way some adolescent boys react. They do not possess manliness; they are obsessed with it.

Such poor reactions may be caused by a deliberately forced separation from the parental home. These boys believe they are free, independent, and capable of self-determination. So they determine themselves—and produce a caricature of a man, similar to the one who falls down the chimney here, looks hideous, and sprawls out.

Hans, too, is not devoid of arrogance, and he is not restrained in his overestimation of himself. He will have to learn.

There is more knocking in the chimney: skulls and skeletons come rattling down and more men "of a hideous appearance" (Bechstein).

What does our hero do? He persists in his new role as a man and greets the macabre company as if he were on the same level, perhaps even trying to play the superior host. "Good evening, gentlemen," he says; then he attempts to flatter them by declaring, "Why, you're complete men, I like that!"

Evidently, there is no reaction, and so he tries the opposite. (He's really not nervous.) He boldly pokes fun at their looks. "Do you belong to the Schön [Beautiful] family?" he says. "Ah, too bad there's no mirror in the room." This is pretty brazen, but it doesn't get him anywhere, certainly not closer to the men. He tries another tack. "How can I be of service to you?" he now asks, trying to ingratiate himself with them (Bechstein). It's no use. The men ignore him and concentrate on playing ninepins with the bones.

Hans's behavior shows how unsure of himself he has become. He reels from one extreme to the other and obviously has no yardstick, no basis for his behavior, no standards and no sense of what to do. He tests, gropes about, and thus offers the typical picture of puberty: the old notions and models have vanished and are rejected, but have not yet been replaced by new ones. Boys of this age live in a no-man's-land. They are lonely and thus try to meet new people; some boys are so desperate that they will make friends with anyone.

Hans was self-critical enough not to join the cats. But the men make an impression on him. He wants to be accepted by them, and he will do anything to gain their acceptance.

No matter how hard he tries, he doesn't make it. At first jovial and patronizing, he winds up acting modest and offering to wait on the visitors. This, too, is typical of puberty: our boys waver between arrogant superiority and unconditional subjugation. For Hans, it turns out that neither mode of conduct is helpful in this situation. The role of the superior lord of the manor does not work. Hans cannot fill these shoes; the part is too big for him. On the other hand, his desire to serve is just as unacceptable. This attitude does not make him the equal of his guests. He would not stand a chance of playing the manly role.

Nevertheless, adolescent boys often go through this phase very intensely and subjugate themselves unconditionally to idols that impress them. They pledge themselves to these idols lock, stock, and barrel, adhere to them unconditionally, venerate them vehemently, and will not submit to any other influence. Practically anybody stands a chance of becoming an adolescent idol, so long as he is outside normal middle-class life. Intellectual or artistic values are not all that necessary, nor do they form an obstacle. Political and philosophical ideologues are just as popular as minor singers. Good looks have less of an appeal. Adolescents do not object to "hideous" looks—or hideous ideas, for that matter.

Our fairy-tale hero is lucky that the men do not accept his offer, do not take him on as a servant. He thus escapes a new dependence, which will get him nowhere. However, he is still on the periphery, and he must hit upon a new and better idea. He says he loves to play ninepins and asks whether he can join the game (Bechstein).

The men, who have already scrutinized him with "dreadful

looks," now grimly ask him whether he has money. Hans, obviously delighted that they are finally reacting and talking to
him, says "*Oui,*" reaches into his pocket and jingles his coins.
The little show-off! Now he wants to show them a thing or
two. He acts sophisticated, *à la française,* and makes it clear that
he knows what to do, not just in regard to ninepins (Bechstein).
Little Hans is putting on the dog. This is in keeping with his
age, and it works so far as the "men" are concerned. He can join
in.

Every boy, or nearly every boy, of this age joins something
that is not consistent with the standards he has been raised by.
He cannot stay out of everything and always remain on the
sidelines, for it is impossible to mature in isolation. Thus, he will
have to conform, adjust to groups, as is customary for this age.
It is altogether a matter of chance which groups he encounters.
He has far less chance of going where he feels drawn than some
parents assume; a sense of belonging depends more on the at-
tractiveness of the groups than on the wishes of individual adolescents. Hans's experience with the cats shows how hard it is
to refuse to take part. He cannot always say no.

This time, he wants to join in, for the group strikes him as so
attractively manly. Yet these "men" are not manly; our hero is
mistaken. However, no one will be able to explain his errors
theoretically or talk him out of committing them. No matter how
convincing the arguments, Hans would turn a deaf ear. Like
anyone else, he has to learn by experience. The maturation process cannot take place in an unconnected way, and the maturing
adolescent will not always succeed in remaining totally clean. So
Hans plays with these hideous people and uses the horrible pins.
He'll survive.

At the very start, he makes sure that he doesn't go under in
this group. He does not uncritically accept what they do, and he
instantly interferes with the events.

"Well, start bowling!" one of the men shouts and hands the
boy a skull. But Hans does not bowl. "Excuse me, but this ball
has corners," he says. "We ought to make it nice and round."

And he promptly sits down at his lathe and makes the "ball" round. Only now does he start to play. Hans bowls well, the men bowl even better, and he loses a bit of money—tuition in the school of hard knocks, so to speak. In the end, he gets a strike— but the clock strikes twelve, the men vanish, and Hans is left empty-handed. He complains. This is understandable, but he has to learn that such experiences are unprofitable. They are not necessary milestones on the road to maturity.

The point is to get through such experiences unscathed. Hans does so by interfering. He does not simply take over the coarse, brutal impulses that are part of this phase. He puts them in a lathe, so to speak, smooths out the corners, shapes them, polishes them. This is how he overcomes those impulses. He is successful. The men stop their din, noise, and howling, they no longer glare grimly, they do not shout at him. He has domesticated them, civilized them. He does to them what his father and the sexton wanted to do to him: he "planes" them and "trims" them. He does all this with the help of the lathe. He learned how to use it at home.

During this stage, many parents may believe that children reject everything and forget everything they have been taught and been given for life. But this assumption is false. Children use and apply the things they have learned, but we frequently fail to notice, for, needless to say, they do not keep us informed.

The next morning, in response to the king's question, Hans says, "I played ninepins and I lost a little money." And he adds that he had fun (Grimm). In the Bechstein version, he declares, "There was a bunch of chimney sweeps here [. . .] and we played ninepins with bones." This is hardly a precise report, and he says nothing about the shaping work he has done at the lathe.

Nor does he mention it to the innkeeper down in the village, even though the man is, understandably, curious (Bechstein). He is so startled by Hans's cool and casual attitude that he feels "thoroughly scared" of the boy. This does not faze Hans. He once again enjoys his superiority and lives it up "on the king's account."

In the evening, he returns to the castle on time. He sits there morosely, murmuring his familiar utterance. Then six "huge men" appear, carrying a bier into the room. Given the plot so far, no one will assume that the hero is frightened by this new event and runs off. We will expect him to act as unscared as ever. But we will also expect him to focus on this macabre procession for at least a moment or, in any case, to look at it briefly. Yet Hans does nothing of the sort. The men aren't even all in the room when he reacts, already knowing what it's all about. "Haha!" he says, overjoyed, "that must be my little cousin, who died only a few days ago." Hans waves his finger and cries, "Come over, cousin, come over!" The men set the bier down before him and vanish.

This reaction is not credible—not by any stretch of the imagination. The unflappability that Hans demonstrates no longer seems genuine or convincing. He is suspiciously hasty in providing a rational explanation for this irrational scene; and his "Haha!" sounds quite out of place. There is, I find, something all too forced about his attempt to make light of the situation. And his explanation is false: no cousin of his has died. After all, we know everything that has happened to Hans during the past few days.

What is the hero trying to cover up? What is he trying to divert our attention from? Is he perhaps more deeply affected than he cares to admit?

If so, he reveals nothing. Without hesitating even an instant, he opens the coffin. A big, cold dead man is lying inside.

But even in making this discovery, Hans does not pause for a second, and he ignores any other feelings triggered by the sight of the corpse. He reacts neither emotionally nor intellectually. Here, where so many questions would be possible, he asks himself nothing, not even who the dead man might be. He evidently switches off his heart and brain altogether and is content to act: he touches the corpse's face, ascertains that he's dead, and concludes, "Ah, he's freezing [. . .], I have to warm him" (Bechstein). In this way, he reduces the extremely unusual and overwhelming event to the simplest level conceivable. Within the framework of this banal assessment of the situation, he finds an utterly harmless part to play: he sees himself as giving friendly help in distress by warming a person who's cold. This is the aim of his actions now: he warms his hands at the fire, then places them on the corpse's face—without success. Next, he takes the body out of the coffin, places it on his lap, and rubs the arms to get the blood circulating. But this does not help either. An idea crosses his mind: "When two people lie in bed together, they keep each other warm." So he takes the corpse to bed, covers it, and lies down next to it. Now, finally, something begins to move. The corpse grows warm, wakes up, and sprawls out. Things get dramatic. "Now I'm going to strangle you!" says the man. But Hans is at no loss for words. With his familiar snottiness, he asks, "Aren't you in a hurry?" (Bechstein). He then grabs the man who has been brought back to such unpleasant life, throws him into the coffin, and quickly screws the lid back on. The six men come and carry off the bier together with its contents. Hans had gotten rid of his problem, but only by the skin of his teeth, I think, and by no means has he overcome it.

If we list all the things he has done with the corpse, then we obviously have a sexual situation. It must have cost our hero a great deal of mental energy not to realize this, to act innocently and find everything quite harmless. The boy who, the previous night, played the sophisticate with his French airs acts as if he doesn't know why two people go to bed together. He acts as if he has no idea that physical contact can lead to erotic contact, and he rubs the arms of his nocturnal bedmate with the professional objectivity of a medical orderly. Furthermore, for his assessment of the scene, he has to believe that a corpse can be brought back to life. Yet previously, at the gallows, he learned that dead men cannot be awakened.

There is nothing believable about Hans's conduct. He becomes genuine and natural again only when the corpse tries to strangle him. He regains his old self-assurance. Previously, he has only been acting superior. He tries to master the situation by retreat-

ing into the role of the innocent, matter-of-fact little boy who
has not yet experienced erotic feelings and, consequently, cannot
be impressed by anything sexual. But he overdoes it. Even a boy
like that would have shown more emotion.

What has so deeply terrified our hero that he believes he has
to shield himself against it? His distress must somehow be connected to the "little cousin"; after all, he talks about him constantly, though without rhyme or reason. He keeps talking about
him and to him, even after seeing with his own eyes that the
corpse is no relative, but a stranger. Nor is he dead, but Hans
regards him as dead. Does he want him to be dead? Then why
does he make such an effort to revive him? What chaos!

These waverings, these dichotomies, are things that Hans wants
to master. He wants to stay in control of the confusing situation,
not show any vulnerability, not be swayed. That is why he sim-
plifies the situation, reducing it to a matter-of-fact level.

There is nothing that boys of his age fear more than emotions.
They are scared of them and shield themselves against them.
To use the jargon of modern adolescents, they want to be "cool."

At one point, Hans must have lost his cool. He must have
reacted, and indeed intensely: toward his (real) cousin. He must
have been emotionally affected by him, and something utterly
new stirred and warmed in him: the desire to touch the boy,
caress him, place his hand on the boy's cheek, lie down in bed
with him.

Presumably, he did not act upon his wish and was forced to
restrain the impulse. That is why the cousin is dead. But now,
in the seclusion of the castle, Hans would be delighted to bring
him back to life. Alone and isolated as he is at this moment, he
yearns for warmth, a warmth that the fire cannot give him. A
yearning is aroused in him for the Thou, the other, who can
release him from his loneliness, whom he can touch, and who
can give him warmth, the warmth of skin, bodily warmth.

Hans's situation is not much different from that of the cats.
They are wretchedly cold, although they have their gang. Hans

is all alone. Hence, he tries to "warm up" a mate for himself. But his effort goes awry.

Hans is confronted not with his cousin, but with his own manhood. Previously, it was in a state of suspended animation. His wishes and yearnings have brought it back to life. Now it gets aggressive and asks Hans who told him to disturb its peace. "No one," should be Hans's reply. No one told him, for he is alone. The new force then threatens him—Hans is faced with dying. The new force is self-destructive, for it has no goal. The energy of mature virility needs a mate. Hans lets the prematurely awakened impulse disappear, for he has no mate to offer it.

Even if we ignore the possible homosexual feelings toward the cousin, we do not see any essentially different picture for Hans's immediate future. Our young hero is not ready for his awakening instinctual tendencies, the need for a mate, for feeling someone else's skin, for going to bed with someone. First, he makes a childishly naive effort to ignore these new feelings; but when they threaten him, he makes short shrift of them and locks them up.

In this scene, he arouses to life something he cannot cope with. He passes the test, because he manages to get rid of the forces he has summoned. He thereby avoids a risk, a disappointment, perhaps a defeat. He gains nothing, but he likewise loses nothing.

However, there is one thing that eludes him: the six men carrying the coffin. He obviously didn't see them; or at least, he ignores them. This is not surprising, from his point of view, for these men are unobtrusive: they don't come banging down the chimney, they don't behave wildly and rowdily, they don't shout, they don't roll their eyes horribly, and they don't play disreputable games. They remain inconspicuous, walk at a measured pace, and do not bluster. Consequently, they do not impress Hans. However, we are told that these are big men, and this is true. They are adults and hence real men. Our hero fails to notice them; they don't fit into his scheme of things.

The same is true of our adolescent sons. They so much want to be men, but not the kind of men their fathers are. They have no eye for or interest in such men, or in anything normal. During this period, their fathers stand little chance of being recognized by them as "complete men."

This problem is shown in the next scene: A terrible giant comes in (Bechstein). He is bigger than anyone else, the Brothers Grimm tell us. He is old and has a long white beard.

Thus, here we have one of the many giants who populate our fairy tales and legends. We wonder where they come from, for it is doubtful whether giants have ever existed on our planet. But this is doubtful only in historical terms. From a child's perspective, the world consists purely of giants. For children, all grownups are bigger, and the biggest is the father. Here he appears with a long beard as the outer sign of his reputation and authority; and, needless to say, he is old. For our adolescents, we are all old.

"Oh, you insect!" he shouts in Grimm; and in Bechstein, he screams, "Worm! Now you have to die!" And he commands: "You must come with me!" (Bechstein).

Understandably, fathers will not put up with scorn and belittlement from their sons. They defend themselves and become aggressive in turn. Yet this is the very behavior to which young people are particularly sensitive; and they hate nothing more than being reminded of their smallness and weakness. During puberty, there are really not many pleasant or positive insights or impressions. However our adolescents do have one thing to be glad of: at last, they no longer see the world from a worm's-eye view, they no longer have to look up to all adults, and they no longer have the daily experience of everyone else's superiority. Often, these boys, now physically as big as or bigger than their parents, seem to be getting their revenge for years of inferiority. When they look back to childhood, it often strikes them as a long period of suppression, and, by these lights, we parents are the wicked suppressors. Our adolescents enjoy refusing to obey.

"I'm not going with you," says Hans. He doesn't act up, he doesn't scream or shout—he doesn't have to. Feeling strong now, he can remain quite casual and declare, "I'm not in any hurry; I have things to do, as you can see." He ignores the "old man" and continues working at his lathe, as cool as can be. The giant tries to grab him. But the giant's beard gets caught in the spindle, which winds in the beard and pulls the head in after it. Hans helps the process along and "treads away briskly." The giant is in his power.

No one will now expect Hans to show compassion toward the old man, and we can understand his gleeful and pleasurable triumph. But the boy goes one step further. "You villain, watch out," says Hans. "I'm going to twist off your big nose and twist out your eyes and twist your thick head into a bowling ball, as sure as my name is Hans." The giant responds with "the finest words" and promises him three chests of gold. "All right," says Hans, but does not free the giant; instead, he makes him carry the lathe on his shoulders and lead Hans to the treasures (Bechstein).

The cruel game that our fairy-tale hero plays with the now-powerless father figure finds very clear parallels in the present age. What harsh and tough criticism today's young people level at their fathers. They attack every last thing, there is nothing their fathers have ever done right. Nevertheless, this younger generation is acting no differently from so many earlier generations of adolescents. They, too, rebelled against their fathers, and frequently against the social systems represented by their fathers; and their protest was no softer or less intense.

External situations and political conditions may change. But the younger generation, their fathers, and the problems between them have always remained the same.

Many fathers have not liked and do not like to see their sons grow up and become more independent and more self-willed. These fathers feel that they do not have to put up with such behavior, and they try to keep their boys small and obedient. They show them how much bigger and stronger, how much more experienced they, the fathers, are, and what worms and midgets the sons are. The result is often fierce competition, with each side convinced that it is the superior. The Grimm version of the fairy tale describes this kind of conflict. "Oh, you insect," the giant cries here, "you'll soon learn what it is to be scared, for you are going to die."

In both versions, the giant threatens the boy with death. He is meant, I think, to die as a competitor. The father wants to force him back into his role as son, as a dependent and an inferior.

This, needless to say, is something the boy does not want. He follows his developmental impulses, which are surging forward. His new energy is still crude and unshaped, of course, and therefore uncivilized. That is why boys of this age are rough, inconsiderate, and often as brutal as the fairy tale depicts Hans. However, a father's reactions are often anything but dainty. "I'm going to grab you!" the giant threatens when Hans remains unimpressed by the giant's entrance. Nor does the boy flinch even now. "Easy now, easy, don't carry on like that. I'm every bit as strong as you," Hans retorts.

His tone sounds familiar, and many adults cannot understand how these boys can have such delusions of grandeur. How can they be so stupid as to imagine themselves the equals of their fathers, who are far older and far more experienced? This is what the giant must be thinking and—in the Grimm version— he suggests a contest of strength. The giant, viewing Hans as a worm, can have no doubt as to who will be the stronger. He takes Hans through dark corridors to a smith's fire, picks up an ax, and smashes the anvil into the ground with one blow. This is indeed a mature accomplishment, and also a marvelous test of manhood. Heroes have matched their strength in this way. The little boy will not be up to snuff. But what does the little boy say? "I can do better than that," Hans declares. This is a stunning example of adolescent braggadocio, and it shows clearly why fathers so readily become hostile toward their sons.

Hans goes over to the other anvil. The old man stations himself next to it, his long white beard hanging down. The boy takes a swing. Naturally, he can't smash the anvil into the ground. He merely splits it. But in so doing, he wedges the old man's beard into it.

For Hans, this is no test of manhood. He does not observe the rules of chivalry like the heroes of olden times; nor does he so much as dream of carrying out a fair joust of strength. He can't afford to do so. If the contest were fair, he would be quite inferior to the old man. Yet he must carry the day in the end; he has to free himself from the old man's authority, from his superior power, which threatens to crush Hans. A boy must become free of dependence—an effort for which he is reproached as much today as in the past. For instance, with statements like: "As long as you're living in your father's house, you have to do what your father says." Wasn't it like this, and isn't it still like this or somewhat similar?

Hans is fed up with this sort of dependence, he has to get out of this situation, and he'll do anything to free himself. All that counts for him is success.

"Now I've got you," says the fairy-tale hero. "Now you're the one who's going to die." From his perspective, the father, as an authority, as a person to look up to, must die. Hans takes an iron bar and keeps beating the old man, until his victim whimpers, begging him to stop.

This, I feel, is not a false picture. Our sons beat away at us quite inconsiderately, though generally with words rather than an iron bar. They know how to hurt us. Furthermore, since they don't abide by even the simplest rules of living together in a sensible way, they usually manage to undermine our authority, wreck our reputations, and demoralize us so thoroughly that we truly no longer regard ourselves as their superiors. In the Grimm version, the giant whimpers, begs for mercy, and promises Hans the greatest riches. In Bechstein, he uses "the finest words" with Hans.

A whimpering father, begging for mercy, is more in keeping with the wishes of certain sons than with reality. On the other hand, there are many fathers who give their sons "the finest words"; indeed, today, they almost exclusively determine the generation scene. For at the moment, youth is "in," and it is earnestly courted on all sides. Fathers particularly excel in this respect. It is chiefly they who take over adolescent views and adolescent jargon, along with certain adolescent fashions, becoming fans of their sons' loud music and feeling or feigning sympathy for their sons' radical political or social convictions. Some fathers have even gone so far as to sympathize with adolescent violence and murder. Rarely, however, is such paternal conduct respected by sons, who frequently reject it as an attempt at ingratiation and put it down with highly derogatory remarks.

A strong and mutually positive father-son relationship is a rare exception during this period. The father's attitude moves between resignation, violent rejection, lack of understanding, and adjustment, while he holds back on his own standpoint. Sons respond in a more uniform fashion. They act out a rebellion against every father, no matter what his attitude. They have to act like this; it is no longer a virtue, for them, to be obedient and well behaved. It would be harmful for them to be deprived of this rebellious phase.

Occasionally, there are good reasons for this loss. For instance, very positive fathers can make sure that their boys do not rebel against them, because, no matter how hard the sons try, they can find nothing to rise up against.

The same thing can happen if the father is too strong. It may never occur to his son to attack him, because the boy assumes that he will simply never get anywhere by rebelling.

The case is no different with famous fathers. It is hard to assail them or put them down, since everyone else recognizes and admires them.

However, even fathers who fail to resist, who put up with and take anything, who give in and offer no opposition, rob their sons of an essential and important experience; they cheat their sons of a process of maturation. For boys need the struggle with their fathers. They have to measure their strength against them and test their powers. In so doing, they get to know their own potentials and limits, they develop their possibilities and gain strength and the capacity to prove themselves.

A boy without a father does not have to forgo this experience. Most boys know how to find a surrogate father to rebel against; if need be, they fight with their mothers.

The conflict between old and young often takes dramatic forms, and not just in the home. Young men also tend to attack any public institution that might be regarded as the equivalent of paternal authority. School, police, the legal system, and, last but not least, the state itself are popular targets; and the methods of attacking them are every bit as undainty as the weapons used at home—on either side.

However, criticism and aggression by young people are not always negative. Thus, their "defiant clothing" added a few original notes to a fashion scene that had slowly gotten dreary. Their "loud music" not only terrified the bourgeois, it aroused a great deal of enthusiasm, knocking many people out of their seats. And new ideas on sex, education, politics, and art have brought some agreeable life and color into the smug world of the bourgeoisie. Thus, the generation gap also has its positive effect. Old and young learn from each other—though neither will admit it, for they confront each other as polar opposites. One side wants to turn the world upside down, the other side is afraid that the world is going to be totally destroyed in the process. The positions are tenaciously defended, and in the end no one wins—nor does anyone lose. The result is a not so disagreeable compromise: the young do not turn the world upside down, nor does the sound world of the old survive as a museum showcase. The world has changed, and this is good, for a thing remains vital only if it changes. Our society has changed in a number of ways: in jurisprudence, in education, in manners and mores. Many of these changes have been forced upon us by the young hotheads—for better or for worse, depending on one's point of view, but this does not matter in this context.

In regard to their personal development, boys always get the better of their adversary. This is shown in the fairy tale: the giant leads Hans to the cellar and gives him the three chests of gold. One, he explains, belongs to the poor, one to the king, and one to him. Then the clock strikes twelve, and the giant disappears. Hans has seen it through. But now the chests seem about to vanish, too. Our hero learns that one cannot rest on one's laurels in this world. Life demands constant struggle and endless alertness. He has evidently understood the lesson, for he does not falter, he remains watchful, and he keeps his presence of mind, holding on to the treasures that threaten to slip away from him. He's made it now. He still isn't scared, but he has released the castle from its spell, freeing the poltergeists and forcing "the enchanted castle into the light." In short, he has "done great things."

And indeed he has, though only "in his own home." For the castle represents the boy's inner realm, the province of his soul, his very being. He has freed himself—from the confines of his egocentricity and autoeroticism. He will no longer focus on warding off urgent impulses and lying in a constant clinch with himself. His cocoon phase is over. He is certainly no beautiful butterfly as yet, but at least he is so free that he can become an endurable social being in human society. This spells new obligations. The chests of gold point to them. Before claiming a reward, he must reward others—first the poor. He thus emerges from his encapsulation, he should and must show interest in his fellow men, commiserate, sympathize, that is, understand other people, even if he is not immediately involved. Giving the chest to the poor means overcoming adolescent self-centeredness. If a boy does not take this step, he will remain stuck here, keep thinking only about himself and viewing as important only the things that concern him. He will never grow up. Contrary to what he thinks, he will never know success, and he will certainly never be happy with his attitude. Keeping the chest that is meant for the poor is economizing at the wrong end. Later on, this is usually deeply regretted, for egoists not only die lonesome—they live lonesome.

In Bechstein, the first chest belongs to the king, that is, the father. The young hero must reeducate himself in regard to him. He has to understand that belittling his father and putting him down were necessary for his own development, but were not in keeping with the objective facts. The father has just as many weak and strong points as the son will have later on. But at present, given his greater experience and maturity, the father often has more strengths than the still-adolescent son. Recognizing his father's weak and strong points is a necessary step in the son's maturing. A sound and successful process of growing up requires the father's "rehabilitation" after the struggle with him. Giving him gold means communicating with him again, not as a child who looks up to him, but man to man. If a son is incapable of viewing his father objectively and thus returning to reality, he will never reach this goal.

Our fairy-tale hero has maintained a positive image of his father: the king. Now that he has made it through all the essential maturation crises, he can transfer the image, both to his own father and, as in the fairy tale, to his father-in-law. The king now becomes the latter. "You have broken the spell on the castle, and you shall marry my daughter," says the king. "That's fine," Hans replies, once again acting more sophisticated than he is or can be. However, he behaves free and self-assured with the king, neither unsuitably servile nor presumptuous. He has delivered his chest of gold to the right place. Hans continues: "But I still don't know what it's like to be scared."

Hans is indeed still naive. And he can be naive; his naiveté is consistent with his age, nor can he be helped in this respect by having overcome personal maturity problems. His naiveté will ultimately be done away with by life, by his concrete experiences, the things he encounters in day-by-day reality.

The king possesses such experience. He is no longer naive, and his answer to the boy proves that the king is a true adult and thus self-sufficient. He is no longer part of Hans's imagination.

"Oh, my dear son and son-in-law," says the king, "just get

married, and everything will be taken care of (Bechstein). Many
men have not known how to be scared, and then they became
terribly scared and couldn't get rid of their goosebumps."

These are the experiences of a man who has no illusions left.
The king's words sound a bit cynical. But Hans doesn't sense
the cynicism; he takes the words at face value and sincerely looks
forward to the prospect of getting married and learning how to
feel scared.

So the wedding takes place. It is a wonderful wedding, and
Hans is very happy. Why shouldn't he be? He is rich now, and
he has a beautiful wife, to boot. But much as he loves her and
elated as he is, he keeps saying, "If only I could feel scared, if
only I could feel scared!"

He has not attained his goal. The things he has gotten were
not the things he wanted, not the things he was striving for; they
fell into his lap. He is certainly delighted, but like a child who
has gotten these things for his birthday. He can't do anything
with them. He is not yet mature enough for marriage, which he
views purely as an institution for learning how to be scared. He
probably loves his wife like a playmate or an especially beautiful
toy. He still has no inkling of what love is. In this respect he
lacks the status of the adult, the man.

This lack may have eluded his wife at first. She must have
found his cheerful, carefree ways quite nice and amusing. But
this is not enough for marriage, for living together. It is not
enough for his wife, it cannot be enough. She gradually gets sick
of his naive chitchat. "In the end, this annoyed his wife," we
read in the Brothers Grimm.

Hans faces his last test. The fairy tale views it as the decisive
one, and this may be true. Many husbands will be frightened by
a woman who makes demands, that is, an unsatisfied wife, who
expects more from them. For some men, this alone can be a
scary situation—beyond their capacity. But something much worse
comes. "He'll be scared, all right," the young queen says to herself, and she has a servant get a whole pailful of gudgeons from
the brook. At night, when the young king is asleep, she pulls off

his cover and pours the pail of cold water and gudgeons over him, so that the little fish writhe about.

The king has come a cropper here, in case he told about his personal experiences. In any event, many men get such powerful goose pimples at this point that they never get rid of them again. No wonder, for a cold shower is probably the last thing they would expect in a situation that has been ubiquitously described as the greatest happiness. Love and bliss are often linked to warmth in a man's emotional realm. Hence, many husbands expect warmth and security as the primary rewards of marriage. They are mistaken. Warmth and security are the prerequisites for a happy childhood. Marriage is an institution for adults, not a rerun of the warmth of the childhood home. A wife is no surrogate mother for bestowing warmth. She has something quite different to offer. And life is not a warm bed, it is bubbly, lively, tingling—at least for those able to free themselves from the attachments and entanglements of childhood.

The yearning for warmth runs through this fairy tale like a red thread. No sooner is Hans out of his home, away from the warm nest, than the problem of freezing crops up. Hans is very cold despite his fire on the gallows hill. He is cold because he is alone. The dead are even lonelier. They rattle and shake in the keen night wind, arousing the boy's pity. Hans takes a fire along into the castle, to keep from freezing. The cats are cold, and Hans also blows on his fire for the half-men so that they won't be cold. The man in the coffin is ice-cold; he is warmed at the fire and in the bed.

Warmth and security are a problem for young people when they leave their parental homes. That's why they huddle together, seeking their lost security with one another. Hans gets beyond this phase and learns the most important prerequisite for adulthood: the ability to be alone. He rings the bell in the spire alone, he sits under the gibbet alone, and he spends the nights in the castle alone. He resists all temptations and passes all trials. He gives to the poor and gives to the king. He has earned his chest of gold honestly. He can dispose of his gold freely. However, he has no use for it as yet. Whom should he give it to, whom should he share it with? He already has everything he needs; he is rich. However, he has not been able to buy the ability to be scared with his chest of gold. So he sighs, he is not really content, and he is worried that he will not be scared even in marriage.

But he will be scared, for now he is no longer alone, and his wife takes the appropriate steps. In the Grimm version, she is assisted by her chambermaid. Presumably, the chambermaid is more sophisticated in this respect, for chambermaids are not watched as strictly as princesses; they are usually more experienced and also more familiar with ways of teaching men to be scared. The princess is smart enough to apply the advice she gets. She pulls the cover off Hans. There he lies, peacefully sleeping, too naive to sense the things that life has in store for him. They are shown to him by his wife, and what he now sees and feels makes his skin crawl and tremble, leaving him dumbstruck. He can only stammer: "At last, now—now I can be scared." The prickly cold water and the teeming life of the many writhing fish wake him up, arousing the man who was in a state of suspended animation within Hans. And now this man can and may live. A completely new dimension of existence opens up to our hero. He feels it and puts his feeling into words. "Oh," he says, "I'm so scared, I'm so scared, dear wife!"

He says, "dear wife," addressing her for the first time; he recognizes her, understands what she means to him, what a keen and vivid sense of life and pleasure she can give him. "Yes, now I know what it's like to be scared," he says, content and virtually released.

The hero's last and thus essential experience is his encounter with the female. He is finally touched by her. She encounters him concretely as a wife and symbolically as a fish pond, in which he thinks he has fallen. This is a world which he was unfamiliar with, ignorant of. This world is new for him, alien, different, exciting. With its waters swirled up by fish, this world is as feminine as his lonely, haunted castle is masculine. These two worlds are as different and as opposite as men and women are. In a fortunate case, the two can achieve the fruitful tensions that lead to mutual enrichment, strengthening and heightening their sense of life.

An important prerequisite for this, as the fairy tale points out, is "being scared." Hans experiences it, gets to know it, in a situation that is (at last) beyond him. He cannot overlook the mob of cold, writhing fish; he cannot keep aloof from them, he is totally at their mercy. He cannot keep the fish at bay, as he has done with everything else, no matter how terrifying it may have been. This is the first time that he is ineluctably affected. Something happens that nothing and no one has previously been able to bring about: neither his father nor the sexton nor the ghosts. This is the very thing he yearned for, the very thing he wanted: to be scared. He went out into the world in order to experience something that would touch him so deeply that he would be "beside himself." That's what he is now. The alien liveliness of the feminine challenges him. He can no longer retreat into himself; he is touched to the quick.

However, this profound effect does not frighten him. On the contrary, he experiences it as a radical stimulus that makes him happy.

He has thus reached his goal. He has taken the final step to maturity; he has grown up. He has overcome the narrow confines of his naive egocentricity; he is capable now of dealing with a Thou, of opening up to the existential other.

The Goose Girl

The story of a naive and arrogant princess, who
feels that everyone should wait on her, who is humbled for this misconception, but who eventually
reaches her goal.

AT THE start of this fairy tale, the heroine does not live up,
or down, to the title. She does not tend geese, does not live in
simple circumstances, and is certainly not in a subordinate position. Not does she have to serve. Quite the contrary: she is
growing up in a rich world, her mother is a queen, and that
makes her a princess. She has everything her heart desires, and
she is beautiful into the bargain. She has been promised to a
prince and can look forward to a magnificent wedding. Her
dowry contains "a great many precious objects and jewels—gold
and silver, goblets and gems." Her mother has given her all this
wealth, "for she loved her child with all her heart," we are told.
Thus, nothing mars the beautiful picture; there are no problems,
the child lives in a peaceful, loving, sound world, and she has
the best prospects for the future.

This is a lovely description. It will appeal to readers young
and old, and they will be delighted at seeing such a girl. No one
will ask whether all this is true to life. Veracity is not expected
here; it is not the responsibility of a fairy tale to be veracious.
And where could you find a girl like this in real life? Just about

nowhere, certainly not in the everyday life of mere mortals. However, life takes place not only in reality. Wishes and fantasies also belong to the reality of our existence, and their realm has such lovely and wealthy princesses. Their wishes for their present and future are just as they are described in the fairy tale. After all, who wouldn't want to grow up in a castle, be one's mother's only and darling child, spoiled and showered with gifts? The fairy tale makes this wish come true. The heroine has no brothers or sisters, and the father died many years ago. As a result, the mother is devoted exclusively to the child and can love her with all her heart. Any possible competition that might interfere is removed. The girl is the sole and unchallenged center of attention. Besides, she has no unpleasant duties to perform in her mother's castle. She doesn't have to help with the housekeeping or take care of any brothers or sisters, much less deal with them. Furthermore, she is beautiful, and her marriage to a prince is in the offing. Thus, the star part is ensured for her not only now, but also for the future.

Such attractive scenery is wished for not only by certain girls. Many parents have similar wishes and dreams. They would love to have a "little princess" as described here, and they do their best to raise their daughters as "little princesses." They spoil them and watch over them, love them with all their hearts, and provide them with all sorts of beautiful things, grooming them, dressing them, adorning them marvelously. And they are proud if other people regard the little girl as something special. And naturally, they wish for a "prince," that is, a man good enough for their little girl. For some fathers, no man is good enough for their "little princess"; they would much rather keep her for themselves forever. Obviously, such daughters enjoy this attention, admiration, and pampering, and they love to play the role expected of them. Most of these girls cannot resist identifying with the role. They believe that they are what they are seen as and what they themselves would like to be. And they not only expect to get a rich and handsome prince later on, they assume that everyone will recognize and respect their role.

Girls are fascinated by this princess image. Parents, other people, many men are equally fascinated. It has a long tradition, and it delighted our ancestors. Nevertheless, it is as unrealistic as a fairy tale. Yet it will take a fairy tale to relentlessly correct this wishful thinking, by showing the realities and describing what the darling little princesses are really like.

At first, however, none of this is noticeable; but then, the princess has not yet left the security of the castle.

The situation changes when she sets out for the other kingdom. The mother does not want her daughter to go without protection. When it's time to say goodbye, the queen goes to her bedroom, takes a "small knife," cuts her fingers, "making them bleed," and lets three drops of blood drip on a white rag. She gives the rag to her daughter and says, "Dear child, take good care of these drops of blood; you will need them on the way."

The daughter may feel the gravity of this action, and she may realize that the rag is something like a heartfelt legacy. So she keeps it on her bosom. But she certainly doesn't stand a chance of comprehending what the mother means, and she doesn't perceive any problems. For the daughter, there is no gap between the beautiful present and her future as a wife at her husband's side.

If her attitude were correct and there really were no problems, then her story would quickly be told. She would travel to her prince, unchallenged, and arrive safe and sound. The wedding would take place in all its magnificence and to everyone's satisfaction. The fairy tale would end after the first paragraph and everyone would live happily ever after. But the transition from the perfect world of childhood to the distant, alien kingdom is not so easy. No girl becomes a woman without encountering problems along the way.

The experienced mother knows this. She knows the difficulties of real life and, one assumes, she should have enlightened her daughter about them, or at least about a few basic facts. She does not do so. Now, at the very last minute, she tries to make up for her failure by means of a solemn, symbolic act. With the three drops of blood on the clean white rag, she minimizes and beautifies the three things connected with blood in a woman's life: menstruation, loss of virginity, and childbirth. The mother does not wish to talk about such concrete physical things; she would like to preserve the pure childhood world of her daughter, keep it intact, shield her against such embarrassing and disagreeable things as sex, blood, and pain.

One can get on the high horse of the modern enlightened person and say that the mother is making a mistake: she should and must tell her child the plain, unvarnished truth about these natural matters. But such a demand would be simplistic. Throughout human history, these three phenomena have been anything but simple and natural. They are fraught with anxieties, superstitions, and taboos. Nothing has made men throughout the world as uneasy and nothing has terrified them as much as this otherness of women, which they did not understand and from which they felt excluded. Men reacted to this situation in their own way. Thus, throughout the world, various nations have viewed (and still view) a menstruating woman as unclean. Women have been envied for their ability to give birth, but they have also been regarded as uncanny for the same reason and suspected of possessing sinister magical powers. These powers were then attributed to their blood, which was said to have supernatural effects. In the past, the blood of a virgin was used as a fetish, and girls who had lost their innocence were ostracized and are still scorned today in many places. We can thus understand the mother's reluctance to discuss these themes, since she would like to protect her daughter against such an unattractive and discriminating reality. Many present-day mothers behave in the same way.

However, the essential significance of the rag is not its symbolic value, but its function of protecting the heroine. The mother would like to remain close to the girl with her blood, help her, and keep speaking to her, even when her daughter is far away. This last task is performed by the three drops of blood.

For further protection, the mother gives the princess a

"chambermaid." The latter is to ride along with her and "deliver the bride into the hands of the bridegroom." The mother hopes that this girl will serve, help, and support her daughter with her special powers and capabilities. A further protection for the daughter is offered by the loyal horse that the queen gives her. Its name is Falada, and it can speak, just as the drops of blood can speak.

Thus, two voices will accompany the princess on her journey: the female, maternal voice of the three drops of blood, and Falada's voice. In mythology and popular superstition, horses are male animals, so we may surmise a paternal element in Falada. Now, the father, we are told, has been dead "for many years." But this does not mean that he has no spiritual influence, especially if the mother keeps his memory alive in the child. The fairy-tale mother here must have done so, since it is she who gives the horse to the princess.

These voices may seem magical, marvelous, miraculous, but they are really nothing special; we all have these two voices at our disposal, and we hear them throughout our lives. They have taken shape in the fairy tale as a rag with three drops of blood and as a horse, and they can speak out loud. Actually, they are inner voices, the voices of Father and Mother. They speak to us long after we have left home and become independent, and even after our parents have passed away. They influence many of our opinions and convictions and affect certain of our actions. They are our conscience and the "voice of blood," which we cannot deny. They do a great deal, but they cannot help us as our real parents did. Once we have left home, we are on our own and we have to figure out how to get along without our parents. Everyone has to do so, and, as we shall see, it is not so easy at first.

It is especially hard for the spoiled and overprotected princess. She cannot believe that she is suddenly defenseless. She thinks that her father and mother are still with her, might still help her and effectively protect her. She also believes that she is a princess. But she is not. A real princess and her precious treasures would never have been accompanied only by a chambermaid; she would have had an escort. Nor would she have had to ride horseback; she would have been driven in a coach. But that's how things work in a fairy tale. All the many grand ladies and gentlemen are normal human beings like you and me—mothers, fathers, and children with very ordinary worries and anxieties.

Nor is the chambermaid a servant. The heroine will bitterly realize this, and soon enough. The costly dowry is just as unreal. The profusion of jewels, gems, and gold could, however, stand for the mother's coddling and pampering of the princess. Notably, not a single piece of the gold ever crops up again in the story. This might signify that coddling and pampering are of no immediate value in the struggle of life. First of all, the consequences of being spoiled and overprotected are negative; such an upbringing creates needs and demands. This is shown right away: the two girls have been riding for only an hour when the heroine feels very thirsty. But instead of dismounting in order to drink, she orders her chambermaid to get her a goblet of water.

One should not hold her demanding behavior against her. She is merely acting on the basis of her previous experience at home, expecting her role to be recognized here, too, and others to wait on her as usual. Her mother certainly would not have refused her request and would not have hesitated to bring her a drink in her golden goblet. But her mother is no longer here, and there is no substitute in life for a pampering mother. The heroine now learns this lesson.

"I don't want to be your maid," says the chambermaid and tells the princess to lie down by the water and drink. Her refusal is followed not by an emphatic exclamation point, but by a plain period. The chambermaid does not make a great to-do about refusing; she simply takes it for granted, just as the heroine takes it for granted that she should be waited on.

The princess is not waited on, and she might readily do without a drink altogether. But she is too thirsty. She is forced to dismount and do something she is unaccustomed to doing: she leans over the water in the brook, drinks, feels sorry for herself, finds it dismal that she can't drink from her golden goblet, and moans, "Oh, God!"

Her perfect world has been nicked.

This kind of shock is something most young people suffer. Such an experience, or a similar one, indicates the end of a protected childhood. A person experiences his solitude, his loneliness; he is suddenly on his own, and he has to cope with life by himself.

Our heroine moans; she cannot believe that this is her new situation and that it will remain like this in the future.

The drops of blood support her self-pity and they lament, "If your mother knew, her heart would burst in her body." This lament is likewise useless for the heroine. She is not equal to the situation. She stands there helpless and does the smartest thing she could do—absolutely nothing. Silently, she mounts her horse again.

The fairy tale calls her humble, but there is no reason to call her this. Bearing in mind that the chambermaid's conduct must be totally unfathomable to her, one may find it remarkable that the princess does not reproach her, and one may see her as somewhat good-natured—but nothing more. The fact is that she has quickly forgotten the "nasty words." This carefree attitude, which is out of place in the situation, demonstrates that she is still a rather naive child. She does not rack her brains about the incident; she merely sweeps the unpleasantness from her mind and hopes that it will not be repeated. She is optimistic, as only a child can be.

There is another way in which she shows that she is still a little girl. After a short time, she is thirsty again and wants another drink. As if nothing had happened, she tells her chambermaid again, "Dismount and bring me water in my golden goblet."

She has learned nothing from the first scene, and this time she insists on drinking from her golden goblet. Her diction is more rigid; neither the word "please" nor any other term of politeness occurs. As calmly as the first time, the chambermaid replies, "Serve yourself if you want to drink. I'm not your maid, whatever you think." The fairy tale says that the chambermaid is speaking "even more haughtily," but there is no evidence of this either.

However, the heroine, who is literally on her high horse, "looking down" on the girl accompanying her, is called humble and is pitied.

Here the description is not objective. The fairy tale sides with the heroine. Its favoritism panders to children. They want clearcut heroes with whom they can identify unproblematically. These heroes must not be criticized, deprecated, or disapproved of. Criticizing is done in all children's lives by fathers, mothers, teachers, and other authorities. No child wants a fairy tale to be a rerun of his daily upbringing. That is why fairy-tale heroes have to be unreservedly good and positive.

Children can delight in this fairy tale, allowing themselves to be loved, spoiled, and showered with gifts together with the heroine in her mother's castle. If they have to leave this cozy environment, then it is only for something better. A magnificent wedding with a rich, handsome prince is a satisfactory alternative. The road to his palace is pleasant if you don't have to walk, if you can ride on a noble steed and have a servant who replaces the pampering mother. And then, something else is attractive: it's fun to order a servant around. Children love this, especially little girls. But here, things get critical, for this fairy tale is responsible not only to children, but also to adults. Parents would never tell a story about children whose conduct they do not consider proper and desirable. Adults certainly don't like arrogant or domineering children. That is why the heroine is not intentionally haughty, and that is why we are assured that she is humble.

However, a fairy tale can certainly describe undesirable and taboo qualities and modes of behavior that are rejected by society; and it can do so without offending anyone. Toward this end, it needs a negative character to oppose the positive hero. All bad and wicked things can be shuffled off on the negative character. This does not hurt, for in the end the negative hero or heroine is punished, usually with death, and thus everything is in order. No one feels disturbed, and the world remains whole and harmonious.

Consistent with this, it is the chambermaid who is haughty and not the heroine. The princess is again pitied. She does not simply dismount from her horse, but the adverb *hernieder* (down) implying grace and elegance, is used. She leans over the water, drinks and weeps, and then moans, "Oh, God!" No new idea comes to the drops of blood, which respond in the same way as before. They cannot help the princess. Perhaps that's the reason, or one reason, why she loses them. In any case, the rag drops from her bosom and floats off with the water. In the appendix to the original version of the tale, the Brothers Grimm say that she has "lost [the rag] innocently." This is certainly true, for she is still a naive and innocent child. This is shown by her unreflected live-for-the-moment attitude when she drinks the water and by her naive carelessness, which leads to the loss of the maternal pledge.

However, it is out of character for her not even to notice the loss. She fails to see what the chambermaid, perched on her horse and much farther away, clearly notices and happily registers. The reason for the princess's oversight, according to the fairy tale, is her great fear. Yet this is never demonstrated. She drinks because she cannot endure her thirst any longer; she is sad because she is not waited on and does not receive her goblet. What should she be afraid of? In her simplicity, she fails to suspect what is about to happen to her. I believe that her great fear is supposed to explain and excuse her failure. No one should dream that the heroine is either terribly stupid or horribly frivolous or that she so much as belittles her mother's weighty gift. As before, the fairy tale keeps the heroine flawless.

Whatever may have caused the loss, it leads to a decisive turning point. The princess is now deprived of all maternal protection; she has become powerless, as the chambermaid quite correctly ascertains. The princess is now forced to be on her own and get

THE GOOSE GIRL 185

along on her own. But she does not realize this as yet. Suspecting no evil, she is about to remount her horse, Falada. But she does not succeed. "I belong on Falada," the chambermaid reveals to her, "and you belong on my nag." The princess's reaction is remarkably calm. Although deeply humbled, she neither weeps, moans, nor laments this time. Nor does she resist, protest, or even lose her temper. Consistent with her previous behavior, she does nothing. We are told, regretfully: "And the princess had to put up with this."

She has to put up with a lot more, because now the chambermaid, using harsh words, orders her to take off her royal garments and put on the chambermaid's poor clothing. As if that weren't enough, she has to swear not to breathe a word of this at the royal court. The princess does not refuse; she swears. Otherwise, we are told, "she would have been killed on the spot." This may or may not be true; in any event, the chambermaid does not threaten to kill her. I regard this explanation as a further excuse for the heroine's behavior.

If we now review the plot so far and ask what the princess has done, accomplished, or excelled in, the results are exceedingly meager. She has let everything happen to her and has never once made the slightest effort to fend anything off; she has not even shown resistance. Her only activity has been to bemoan her fate. She has displayed no special qualities, peculiarities, or characteristics, not even negative ones, for she was not aware of her arrogance. Hence, she does not even have defects and is ultimately bland and dull.

One must ask how she comes to be the heroine of this story. And what sort of heroine is she anyway? Who would like a girl like this?

No doubt, the mother likes her daughter. After all, it was she who raised her in this way, making her into a "little princess."

Did she do it with a thought to the prince whom the girl was to win and, consequently, would have to attract? Did the experienced old queen know what men like and what they wish for? Does the heroine fit some kind of widespread male ideal? Do men like such girls? Perhaps the queen mother reasoned as follows: Her daughter is beautiful, that's important to them. Nor does she stint with her dowry, which is advantageous. Perfection is popular, so the princess has no failings or shortcomings. She can be a little pallid and boring; indifference is scarcely a minus factor. Weakness and helplessness are distinct advantages, highly suitable for winning a man's love. Men, as the strong sex, like the opposite, but not competition. Hence, they are not so keen on intelligence in women; they may *respect* a critical female mind, but they won't love it. Activeness and initiative shown by a woman are less desirable, because they can shake a man's ego. Personality in a woman is not important for such men; after all, they have their own personality. And why should a girl make her own way? Might she not ultimately try to *get* her own way with the man? This is a disagreeable idea for him. Such a man likes his peace and quiet, he doesn't want a power struggle, he would much rather protect the woman with his strong arms. And he likes to wage the struggle of life for her. He regards strength and struggle as *his* forte; a woman doesn't need these qualities. On the other hand, she is granted the right to be sad and weep occasionally—the man likes to comfort her. The important thing is that she can subordinate herself, that she do what he tells her to do, that she submit to him. He does not appreciate resistance or rebellion; he does appreciate female humility. He does not expect her to have ideas of her own; only men can have them, he feels. He, the strong and active man, seeks the devoted, passive, female opposite in her.

This interpretation of the gender roles may be viewed as old-fashioned by many people and rejected. That's fine, and I would go along with these people unreservedly. Nevertheless, caution is recommended, and we must bear in mind that this image of male and female is extremely old, deeply embedded in tradition, and therefore profoundly rooted in our minds. It cannot be argued away. The most enlightened rationalist and the most inveterate feminist are not free of this conception. They will occasionally fall prey to it and then be extraordinarily shocked when they are forced to realize that it is easy to advocate a modern, emancipated position, but far more difficult to live by it successfully. They can no more avoid conflicts in living together than their less progressive contemporaries; often, their relationships have considerably more problems. I fear that we are all burdened with this worldwide conception of gender roles.

Our fairy tale presents not just one version of femaleness. A second one is depicted in detail, and this version is neither attractive nor flawless: the chambermaid. If we observe her conduct, we see that she is neither helpless nor passive. She also has ideas, though negative and wicked ones, and she has enough gumption and initiative to act on her ideas. She heedlessly ignores decency, moral standards, and ethics. Her rejection of obedience is spontaneous and natural, and her refusal involves a carefully measured show of strength.

An acute observer, the chambermaid discovers the princess's weakness and exploits it to her own advantage. Nor does she stop at halfway measures. She is not content with taking the horse—she takes everything she can get. She exploits the situation totally and has no inhibitions.

The chambermaid is not only capable of getting her own way, she is also ruthless and, we are told, uses nasty words. She uses harsh words to threaten the princess. She is successful in refusing to play the part of a maid and instead usurps the role of a princess.

The fairy tale, of course, neatly separates the two girls into good and evil. The heroine is depicted as positive, the chambermaid as negative, which implies that they have nothing in common. But if we refuse to draw this demarcation line, if we add up their qualities, seeing both girls together as two sides of one person, we come to a somewhat more realistic picture of a girl.

If the princess's pattern of behavior corresponds to an embellished ideal, the chambermaid's conduct is altogether different. It will strike an unpleasantly familiar chord in any parent with an adolescent daughter. The fairy tale spares the feelings of such harried parents by making the behavior toward the princess so ugly. Actually, an adolescent girl frequently aims such behavior specifically at her parents. At home—and more and more at school—teenage girls are developing this sort of activity and initiative typical of their age. They have a lot of ideas during this period and no inhibitions about acting on them. They are sharp observers and seem well versed in our weaknesses. Once they know where to apply pressure, they seldom stop halfway, they normally exploit a situation to the full. Ruthlessness is characteristic of adolescent rebellion.

Naturally, teenage girls don't like to obey, and they have their own, specifically girlish way of disobeying. They refuse to listen or submit, as if this refusal were their unqualified inalienable right. And in many other respects as well, one can see that modesty is not their forte. The pride and arrogance of some girls would be fascinating if their irritating behavior didn't get under our skin.

The heroine of our story has skipped this phase of development. She has not gone through a rebellion at home and never attacked her mother. She has never criticized her, but instead has gratefully taken everything her mother has given her. Hence, she lacks the experience of such conflict. She has remained naive and callow; nor can she defend herself or get her own way outside the house. She is no match for someone like the chambermaid. She seems weak and totally unheroic in their confrontation.

Nevertheless, the princess does have her strong sides. At the high point of her humiliation, she does not do what one might expect her to do, given her previous crybaby attitude: she does not run home to mother in order to seek protection and help. She does not even make the attempt, does not even consider it. Now that she is really in a bad way and has lost everything, she does not even complain, she does not moan, weep, or lament. She puts on the poor clothing, climbs on the "nag," and doesn't even seem angry at the chambermaid, for, we are told: ". . . and then on they rode, until at last they arrived at the royal castle." It almost sounds as if there were no friction between them.

A pampered upbringing, such as the heroine has enjoyed, certainly has its advantages. Of course, it doesn't give a child a competitive edge out "in the street," in the relentless struggle among peers. Spoiled children don't stand a chance here. They are regarded as weak and are exploited and belittled. They suffer humiliation and defeat. However, it is wrong to see these failures as portending a negative future. It is wrong to criticize these children all the time and demand that they prove their mettle. Often, "little princesses" or "mama's boys" who have been horribly made fun of do not have less chance of making it in life. On the contrary. And this contrary situation is shown in the fairy tale. It is not the cunning and superexperienced chambermaid who attains her goal in the end, but the previously so unassuming princess.

Tender pampering and friendly affection between parents and children create a vast latent strength in children, sometimes making them superior to other children. However, these spoiled, coddled children need more time to develop; they evolve their potential somewhat later. For many of them, success seems to drop into their laps, while the people who seemed to have the upper hand as children are frequently unable to maintain their dominance, and stay trapped in mediocrity or even fail altogether. They draw the wrong conclusions from their initial successes and overestimate themselves.

This is the very mistake that the chambermaid makes. She has an easy time of it with the heroine. She must think the world of herself for so easily getting the better of a princess! She probably considers herself at least as strong and powerful as her mistress. In any case, that's how the chambermaid acts, and she believes that only the horse can endanger her usurped position. She is wrong. To be sure, we are told that Falada "saw everything, and he remembered it." This sounds as if the noble animal were about to interfere in the events in order to rescue and avenge the princess. However, the chambermaid manages to prevent this. She will bring about her destruction by herself, above all because she overestimates herself.

Her first success is made possible by the heroine's loss of the rag and thereby of her maternal protection. The chambermaid respects the mother; she even fears her in the guise of the rag and does not dare mistreat the daughter. For the heroine, the rag means that she may feel as protected and secure as if her mother were still with her. But sooner or later, people have to learn how to get along without their parents. This step toward independence is highly essential as well as difficult and painful; at first, however, it spells only loss and renunciation.

The heroine does not realize this as yet; she does not even notice that she has lost the rag and that a highly decisive "die and be renewed" scene is taking place over the flowing water of the brook: the heroine dies as a person who identifies unreflectingly with her mother and is dependent on her. This is where her childhood phase ends, and, as if reborn, that is, helpless and unprotected, she is now exposed to life. This new life has nothing in common with her previous existence as a child in the castle. Life outside proves to be harsh and relentless. She suddenly loses everything that she has previously possessed, and now she becomes a ruthlessly exploited victim. However, this oppressive situation first reveals the heroine's latent strength: she is equal to this challenge and does not lose her nerve or her head. Although spoiled and demanding, she can take punishment and endure hard times without complaining. This girl is not easily shaken.

Such a high degree of mental stability is very helpful in life and hence an educational goal that is worth striving for. However, modern pedagogy would criticize the way the mother in this fairy tale deals with her daughter. Today's pedagogy does not care for the naive, well-behaved, conformist child; it wants critical and emancipated children. It refuses to transfigure reality with beautiful symbols; it prefers rational enlightenment and concrete information.

Such an upbringing certainly has its advantages; but we doubt that our children, with their modern upbringing, possess the stability and self-confidence that the heroine of this fairy tale reveals. Nor are our children as calm, as friendly, or as unsuspecting. Often, their relationship to their parents is not this positive, and many of our children are something that the heroine is not: aggressive.

All extremes in education have their defects. Thus, the loving, coddling mother in the fairy tale is very one-sided. She may give her child inner strength and security, but she does not enable her to make her own way. No sooner is her daughter exposed to crude reality than she comes a cropper.

She sits no longer on Falada, but on the chambermaid's nag, wearing the servant's inferior clothes. And the princess then has to watch as the king's son welcomes the chambermaid, instead of her, with "great joy" and leads her up the stairway. The princess has to remain outside. Meanwhile, the old king looks out the window, sees her in the courtyard, and observes how "fine" she is, how "delicate and beautiful."

Her qualities are not tied to externals, nor does the situation, which is so discouraging for the heroine, change her in any way. She maintains her bearing, does not reveal herself, and does not accuse the chambermaid. She accepts her misfortune because she feels responsible about keeping her word.

One may regret that she acts in this way; one may regard it as unsensible and anything but "normal"; but that's what she's like. She is not practical, certainly not opportunistic; she is moral. She observes the standards and values that she has been brought up to respect.

Her conduct is the result of her "royal" upbringing. Weak educators and a permissive, pluralistic education do not produce this sort of attitude.

The old king would like to know who the maid is. He goes to the royal chamber and asks the bride about her.

This is the first time that the chambermaid must answer questions in her new role. Not hesitating for even a second and without the slightest loss of confidence, she says, "I took her along on the way, for company; give the maid some work to do so that she won't stand around idly."

The chambermaid does not think about how she ought to act as a princess in order to meet expectations. She speaks and behaves as she is used to doing. Even her diction corresponds to her standing; it is casual. No princess speaks in such a casual way, nor would she ever take along a strange girl whom she had met en route; she would at least know her name. And how does the false bride treat the old king, her future father-in-law? She exhibits no respect whatsoever, is not even courteous, and is certainly not friendly. She orders him around, nor does she answer his question.

In the royal chamber, the response to her inappropriate conduct is peculiar. The two kings do not even exchange astonished looks. They are not indignant, not amazed, not embarrassed. It never even occurs to them to send the ill-bred young queen back to her mother. Nor do they nurture any doubts about who she is. They do not test her in any way; they do not even ask the girl in the courtyard who she is or where she comes from. They believe whatever the strange princess tells them, and the old king, like a well-behaved child, does what she tells him to do. He has no work, knows of none, we are told, but he then says, "I have a little boy who tends the geese. She can help him."

The second example of the chambermaid's conduct is offered to the young king: "Dearest husband, please do me a favor," she says, and these are her only friendly words. She does not say them out of love or affection, nor in order to be tender or to please the prince. She is friendly only in order to get him to do what she wants. He promises to do it. "I'd be glad to," he replies. Assured of his promise, she now strikes a different tone: "Well, then, call the flayer and have him cut off the head of the horse that I rode here, because it annoyed me during the trip."

The prince is offended by neither the form of her request nor the content. He is not disturbed by the fact that she is taking out her whim on an innocent horse, nor is he frightened by her unrelenting harshness. He, too, does what she tells him to do. He calls for the flayer. Falada must die.

The chambermaid has not changed in her new role; she instantly makes use of her new power. No sooner is she in the castle than the old king and the young king obey her every wish. She shows that she can get her way not just with the naive and helpless princess. She demonstrates her dominance toward two strong men and makes them dance to her tune.

Unchallenged and undoubted, she plays her part as mistress, even though she makes no effort whatsoever to make her role sound genuine and convincing. For after the prince has accepted her as the princess and led her up the perron into the castle, her beautiful clothes are the only things that truly recall a royal background. The chambermaid does not try to act noble or educated, nor does she give anyone a reason to view her as well bred or charming, much less noble and good. Heedless of the expectations that others may have of her, she is true to herself: cold, harsh, ruthless, and domineering.

Nevertheless, she achieves what she is after. She gets her own way, usurping the role of the princess and becoming the prince's bride. She allows the men neither to dominate her nor to tell her anything. She is the one who determines what happens.

The real bride and true princess has no say now. She does as she is told, becoming a poor maid who tends geese. She learns that Falada has been killed. With the shameful death of her loyal horse, she has lost the very last thing tying her to her mother and the family castle. Now she is all alone and without a friend in the world. The last witness to her noble background has died with Falada. She must therefore bury any hope of rehabilitation. Her situation appears hopeless. Nevertheless, she does not despair, nor does she hate her chambermaid, even though she knows that the girl is responsible for the poor animal's death. She secretly goes to the flayer and pays him to nail Falada's head on the dark gate, through which she has to pass every day with the geese. She wants to see the horse frequently.

Every day, she shows her grief under the dark gate. "Oh, you, Falada, hanging there," she addresses the horse's head, and it answers, "Oh, you maiden queen when you went, / if your mother knew, then her heart would be rent." It is a sad scene, and it makes us feel sad. Some children who hear it get tears in their eyes. Even though Falada speaks, everyone knows he is dead. He hangs under the dark gate, where no one else can see him. He can no longer act in the princess's life. She is alone, even though she talks to him. It is virtually a graveside dialogue. She then silently leaves the town, we are told.

The reader feels sorry for the heroine and is angry that she is treated so wretchedly and her evil adversary so nicely. Why does the goosegirl deserve such a bad fate? She has none of the wicked qualities of the chambermaid. She never lies, never cheats, never hurts anyone. She is decent, friendly, sympathetic, and virtuous. But what good are all these fine traits? Where do they get her? Ever since she left home, her life has gone very poorly. She has lost everything she possessed, been demoted from a princess to a maid, is mistreated, pushed around, and must finally tend geese. She has reached the lowest rung of the social hierarchy and has almost no prospect of changing this status.

She takes it all, she puts up with it. Her almost absolute passivity is interrupted only when she bribes the flayer; but this bribe cannot change her lot, any more than her dialogue with Falada's lifeless head can. Her reasons here are purely sentimental—or so it seems.

Despite all her misfortunes, the scene out on the goose meadow does not seem somber. No sooner does she arrive than she "sits down and loosens her hair." She evidently ignores her goose-tending, which she leaves to Kürdchen. But he sits down on the job, too. He watches her with keen interest and is delighted at her shiny hair, for it is "pure gold." However, he doesn't stop at silent admiration; he wants to "pull out a few of her hairs."

Given her previous passivity and her constant inferiority, given the way she has put up with everything, one ought to assume that she will now give up several of her golden hairs. But this is not the case; nor does she tussle with the goose boy. She has no trouble keeping him at bay when he makes an awkward boyish attempt to move in on her. She says:

Woe, woe, little wind,
Take Kürdchen's little hat,
And make him chase it,
Until I've braided up my hair
And put it up again.

A wind does come, and it is so powerful that it blows away Kürdchen's hat, forcing the boy to run after it. The girl can braid her hair in peace, and she is finished by the time he returns. He has nothing for his trouble—he can't pull out a single hair from her head. He is so annoyed that he feels angry and refuses to talk to her.

Our heroine has suddenly developed marvelous abilities. She knows an incantation for the wind, and it works—all laws of nature to the contrary. She commands forces that one would never think a human being capable of influencing. The things she does here are not natural, fit into no framework, and cannot be explained with the aid of reason or science. But they work.

Ages and ages ago, wise women were thought to have these abilities. But of course, they did not possess such magical powers; they were overrated. Our heroine likewise cannot control the wind. But what she does achieve is no less remarkable; it is equally unnatural and inexplicable: Kürdchen, who stares at her and wishes to pull out a few of her hairs, instead runs after his cap like a fool. He does something he does not want to do, and there is only one reason for it: *she* wants it. She gets her way without much effort, merely sitting there, combing her hair, and pronouncing an incantation. That's all.

The reader believes that the situation forces the heroine to make the boy chase his hat. We assume that her magic is defending her against his presumptuousness. But we are wrong. She quite intentionally provokes him, for she could have combed and braided her hair in the privacy of her room. Yet she does not do so. She plays an age-old feminine game with the boy, three times in a row. First she attracts him, then she gives him the brush-off. It is amazing that he is taken in again each time. He does not learn from his experiences, he does not become any wiser, and he goes racing after his cap even the third time. Yet all he had to do was hold on to it.

It's easy for an outsider to talk, to assume that something this silly would never happen to him. But we are not in the situation ourselves. We do not see the girl combing her golden hair, we do not see it shining in the sun, nor do we hear her voice. Hence, we are not in Kürdchen's state, a state in which neither age nor experience protects us. We are not bewitched, bewildered, or whatever.

A German poet was so impressed by this scene in the field outside the town, he found the heroine's charming feminine game so appealing, that he turned the goosegirl into verse. Heinrich Heine writes in *Deutchland, ein Wintermärchen* (Germany, A Winter's Tale), chapter 24:

> *How my heart did beat when the old woman*
> *Told me about a king's daughter,*
> *Who sat lonesome on the heath,*
> *Grooming her golden hair.*
> *She had to tend the geese over there. . . .*

This "tale from olden times" haunted him, as did the golden hair, which he gave to Lorelei in one of his best-known poems:

> *She combs her golden hair.*
>
> *She combs it with a golden comb*
> *As she sings a song;*
> *The song has a wondrous,*
> *Powerful melody.*

Heine knew about the highly effective, magically feminine powers; having often experienced them personally and bitterly, he was familiar with their "powerful melody." His poem tells of what happens to the poor boatman. Even though the girl is far away, high on the rock and doing nothing but combing her hair and singing, the man in the boat is spellbound. Because of the "most beautiful maiden," he forgets to steer, ignores the reefs, and then, instead of achieving the bliss he hopes for, he is devoured by the waves.

The story has a classical model: the shores of an Aegean island are covered with the bleached bones of stranded Greek sailors. The charming song of the sirens lured them into death.

In point of fact, however, feminine magic has never been so homicidal. Yet men have believed that it *was* murderous, and since time immemorial they have wavered between fascination with and terror of the opposite sex. Thus, throughout human history, times of great admiration for women have alternated with times of cruel persecution of women. Had the goosegirl lived in such an era, and had Kürdchen told about what she did to him and the wind, then she might have been burned at the stake as a witch.

In a world generally ruled and determined by men, it was quite natural that women developed certain powers and talents as strategies for getting their own way. Their tactics do not resemble those of men and cannot be seen through or understood by them; yet they are so effective that women can often get their men to do or say what they themselves wish.

These abilities are not linked to class, descent, or education. The simple chambermaid makes the two kings do what she wants, and the princess makes Kürdchen chase his cap against his will. One girl does it with erotic charm, the other without it—but both succeed.

However, the goose girl gains nothing from her cat-and-mouse game with the boy. All she manages to achieve is to prevent him from pulling out her hair. Making him run across the meadow does not change her situation in any way. But this is not her goal. At least, she does not think about her situation. She does not rack her brains, does not forge any plans, does not seek any solutions. Every day, Falada's head says to her, "Oh you maiden queen," thus reminding her of her true status. But she does not react; she seems to be resigned to her situation, remaining passive and unimaginative, as girls are often said to be.

Nevertheless, something does happen. The second time that Kürdchen is so perfidiously forced to chase after his cap, he is not only angry and no longer on speaking terms with her, he goes to the old king and complains: "I do not want to tend geese with that girl anymore," he says. And when asked for an explanation, he tells everything, repeating verbatim the princess's dialogues with the horse's head.

From here on, things run their course. The king eavesdrops on the goose girl at the dark gate, and he watches Kürdchen chasing after his hat for the third time. That evening, the old king invites the princess to visit him. He asks her why she does all these things. But she tells him nothing even now. "I cannot tell you," she replies. "I cannot lament my fate to any human being, for I have sworn an oath under the open sky. Otherwise I would have lost my life." He insists, leaves her no peace, but he can't get a word out of her, we are told.

She truly has a chance here, and it is most likely her last chance. She could now finally change her fate, for the old king would unquestionably believe her after everything that he has heard and seen. But she holds her tongue rather than take advantage of the opportunity; she does nothing for herself. She is either too good for this world or too stupid and too naive ever to achieve any success in life. At least, so the reader is convinced, given the situation, and we cannot believe in any miracle now. Nevertheless, the improbable, the incredible, occurs. She never has to tend geese with Kürdchen again. Her role as goose girl is finished. She is fully rehabilitated, everything ends happily for her, and she also gets her prince.

Is this sheer chance, undeserved luck, to which she has contributed nothing, indeed, which she has almost prevented? Or was her inactivity merely feigned? Did she actually work out a cunning plan, which she carried out ingeniously?

None of this is true. She is neither too good nor too stupid, she has not made a plan, and she has had no tactical ideas. These are typical forms of male behavior. That's how men solve their problems: they ponder, plan, and then act, and are constantly aware of their goals and their actions.

Naturally, she could have done likewise. This ability is not limited to men; women have it, too. But the path she chose was altogether different; she went her own, very feminine way. This course, however, was possible only for her and is closed to men.

What she did has nothing to do with tactics, it is absolutely not an intrigue, not an action, and is difficult to explain.

She did not consciously annoy or anger Kürdchen, hoping that he would then go to the old king. Nor did she deliberately spend so much time in front of Falada's head so that the boy would hear everything. But still, she did do these things, and she gave him the chance to eavesdrop. He most likely heard her dialogue twice, for he could repeat every word; yet she did not act according to a plan.

When she speaks to the old king, she certainly does not choose her words carefully, and she has no specific goal in mind when she says, "I cannot lament my fate to any human being." Presumably, she did not place any special stress on the words "human being." Nevertheless, it occurs to the king that she could lament her fate to the iron stove.

She does so. Nor does she compromise herself by doing it; she can answer to her conscience. She does not break her word.

So she climbs into the stove and begins "to moan and weep, pouring out her heart." She tells everything, the entire story.

This is her salvation. She is then instantly dressed in her royal garments.

She has not consciously planned a single one of the steps that have led to the happy end; she has done nothing deliberately. Yet none of this is mere chance. Her few active efforts, which, so far as we can see or logically assume, do not seem apt to help her, nevertheless get things going. Bribing the flayer, conversing with Falada, playing her game with Kürdchen—these actions necessarily lead to further actions. Between unawareness and purposeful chance, she manages to influence events in her favor.

If we look back at her conduct, everything she does seems extremely goal-oriented. She makes no mistakes, nor does she settle for less than she wants. She wants everything, just as the chambermaid wanted everything. She proves to have made the right choice in not telling the old king anything. Not only is she rehabilitated, but her virtue remains spotless: she refuses to break even a forced promise. She achieves the best possible result.

From a male perspective, however, her behavior would be seen as very hazardous, a gamble, in which she risks gaining nothing. If she had lost, she would have had to go back to tending geese, presumably for the rest of her life.

However, the male perspective is a useless standard for female conduct.

The heroine does not indulge in a single "masculine" reflection. She does not weigh the risks, and she does not picture what might or might not happen. She is not made to waver by thinking. Her actions are always spontaneous. She does not need to take a detour through the conscious mind. One could put it most simply by saying that she is guided by her feminine intuition. She instinctively knows what men are all about. That is why the heroine can readily hold her tongue and leave everything to the experienced old king; she is quite convinced that he will hit on something. And indeed he does. He gets an idea, for men always find a way out of such situations. It is not for nothing that they are considered intelligent in this area, and girls know that men are intelligent.

We must now discuss the crucial scene with the stove. Here, too, the princess is not putting on a show, hoping that someone is eavesdropping. I believe that she is quite certain that someone is listening, because, consciously or not, she has seen through the king's trick. Besides, girls do not lament and yammer, nor do they pour out their hearts when they are alone. Furthermore, our heroine is not astonished, not even surprised, that the royal garments are brought to her the instant she leaves the stove.

The goose girl's complete success speaks for her feminine method, or whatever one would call what she does here; there isn't even a word for it. But in any case, this talent is not an improbable fairy-tale figment. Regardless of age, beauty, and outer circumstances, nearly all female creatures possess these highly effective abilities. Men do not have them, do not know them, cannot truly feel them, and do not know how to cope with them. The capabilities of both our fairy-tale heroines are universal female capabilities. That is why what happens to the two kings and the boy Kürdchen in this story happens more or less to all men. Whether young or old, poor or rich, female wishes and female "magic" influence men's intentions and behavior (especially their marriage plans) and also some of their actions. Our fairy tale shows this: the heroine wins out despite the worst possible prospects. She now stands there in her royal garments, and her beauty, we are told, seems miraculous.

The old king sends for his son and reveals to him that he has the wrong bride, who is only a chambermaid. And he shows him the right bride. The prince is impressed and ecstatic when he sees the former goose girl's "beauty and virtue." He instantly orders a "great feast," inviting "all people and good friends."

He can show this girl to his friends and also present her in public. She sits at his side. The chambermaid sits on the other side. But she is dazzled and fails to recognize the princess in her "radiant adornment."

Indeed, the chambermaid is blinded in a number of respects.

First of all, she believes that she is the prince's legitimate wife, and she feels secure in this position.

This is a poor assessment of the true situation, for she is anything but secure, and she is mistaken about her status. She is not the prince's wedded wife. He certainly welcomed her with great joy, bounding toward her, helping her down from the horse, and leading her up the stairs. But that was all. She was not introduced to his friends or to all the people at court. She vanished into the royal chambers. Here, she addresses the prince as her husband: "Dearest husband, please . . ." But what does that mean? He did not ask for her hand, there was no feast, and certainly no wedding. She is always described as his bride.

The chambermaid doesn't care. She plays the mistress all the same, never making any effort and thinking only of her own goals and plans, which she pursues successfully. She is never described as beautiful, and she is certainly not "fine" or "delicate" and anything but sensitive.

The high point of her negative behavior is her treatment of Falada. What she asks for and what she does goes against everything that one expects of a woman, especially a bride. With no trace of feeling, she coldly and brutally demands: "Have the horse's head cut off."

One might forgive her for her deception and for her behavior toward the princess. But one cannot forgive her cruelty toward the defenseless animal. This deed merits a wretched end, especially in the eyes of children.

Until then, she does nothing to mitigate her crimes. She remains unqualifiedly true to her negative stance, never relenting one bit, never changing; she virtually paints herself into a corner, evoking her own doom.

The old king gives her a riddle. He describes all her evil deeds and asks her, "What judgment does she deserve?" Without hesitating, the chambermaid replies, "She deserves nothing better than to be stripped naked and put in a barrel lined with sharp nails; and two white horses have to be harnessed to the barrel and they will drag her to her death, from street to street."

She has sealed her fate. "That woman is you," says the old king, "and you have named your own judgment, and it shall be carried out on you." It is done. The chambermaid dies, leaves the scene, and no one will shed a tear for her. On the contrary, everyone will be delighted that the princess has now been freed from the wicked chambermaid.

Wondrously beautiful, fine, delicate, flawless, and virtuous, the heroine survives. The young king marries her, his "proper wife," and the two of them rule their kingdom in peace and happiness. That's what the final sentence tells us.

The fairy tale ends in lovely harmony. The outcome is liberating and satisfying for everyone.

I am sorry that I have to retouch this beautiful picture. But the mistake is obvious: a girl like this does not exist. At best, angels have these qualities, and even their existence is arguable.

In any case, they don't exist on earth, and no citizen of earth is granted the joy of living with a spouse in lasting peace and pure bliss. These are facts that everyone knows.

Of course, it takes men a long time to realize the truth. They will not be quick to give up the joy of possessing a "princess." As though they were deaf, dumb, and blind, they overlook, block out, and ignore anything that does not fit into this beautiful picture. This "blindness" is practiced by the two men in our story. The chambermaid's behavior may be remote from that of a princess, but the two kings put up with it. They are never assailed by doubts; they obey her almost slavishly.

But as soon as they realize their mistake, they go to the other extreme and find nothing positive in their onetime idol. She is unmasked through trickery, decried as a swindler, and disposed of. Such women should not exist.

In this case, as in similar cases, which occur daily, somewhere or other, it is not the girl who does the deceiving. The man does the deceiving: he deceives himself. It is he who projects angelic qualities into a women and, contrary to all reason and logic, expects an angel. The inevitable disappointment makes him angry, unjust, and cruel—not only in fairy tales. After all, there is not a single rational reason why women should be either angels or devils. They are neither. Both notions are wrong; these extremes are one-sided.

They are as wrong and as one-sided as the two girls in our fairy tale. Neither girl is natural or real. Neither the princess nor the chambermaid exists. Human beings, girls, are never as good and positive as the princess or as evil and negative as the chambermaid.

Unlike many fairy-tale heroes, the princess and the chambermaid have no names. This is understandable, for they represent only aspects of the female. They are parts of a whole and do not appear separately. They belong together.

Several things point to this. They ride away from the castle together, and they ride together even after exchanging roles. Both sit on Falada and on the nag, both are a maid and a princess, and both are the prince's brides. They possess all important things jointly, even the golden goblet. Both girls can manipulate males, and both are arrogant. In the end, the chambermaid misjudges the situation as badly as the princess did at the start, and the chambermaid turns out to be just as naive when she unsuspectingly stumbles into the trap. At the very end, she even represents the princess's morality and virtue. She harshly condemns all the evil deeds and demands the worst punishment for the evildoer.

In the fairy tale, she dies for her misdeeds. This is a trick to have an artificial happy ending. It is wonderful that the heroine radiantly survives, while her evil adversary is shunted aside forever. Yet this is not true. The chambermaid lives on, in the princess as in every girl, every woman. This is the reality.

The angelic nature of many girls, their princess character, is as external as the good behavior of many female children. Thousands of years have crystallized this conduct and this bearing as expedient. Girls display them in everyday life, and also in fairy tales and literature. The goose girl corresponds to this image, as does her literary sister, Lorelei.

Heine's idyll of a golden-haired girl on a rock over the Rhine is still known and sung today. This is not due to Heine's lovely verses. Brentano's verses were no less skillful, but his Lore-Lay is far less popular. She has too many characteristics, she has a destiny and a story. Heine's Lorelei has none of these things. She is beautiful, wondrous, a virgin, she combs her hair and she sings. What more do we need! Men are thralls to this image: they allow themselves to be devoured by the waves, and they do the stupidest things. Naturally, they would love to possess a girl like this, and this means: marry her.

This is the crux of the matter. This is why girls like to flaunt beauty, virtue, passivity, and a lack of characteristics. This is how they attract princes. If a man is fascinated with this image of a girl, then he does not ask a lot of questions, he tests neither himself nor the woman, he stops thinking, loses his critical faculties, and all he wants to do is have her. We see this happen in everyday life. And it happens in fairy tales, too: the prince knows nothing about his wife. He does not know her, has no inkling of her character, her nature, her qualities. She is promised to him from far away. She comes from a castle; she is a princess. That's enough for him. No questions are necessary. No doubts or qualms. He welcomes her joyfully and takes her into his castle.

She turns out to be the wrong bride. But the next bride is right there. He learns that she is the real princess, and he already admires her beauty and virtue and marries her with no further ado. He knows nothing else about her either. He marries an ideal, in which he believes, but which does not really exist. Actually, he also marries the chambermaid, for she is a component of the princess.

A girl as good and flawless as the princess would be unable to survive in this world, in which everyone has to defend himself and make his way. The princess therefore needs the chambermaid's qualities and abilities in order to survive. These traits are negative only in isolation. Imbedded, steered, and concealed by feminine charm and feminine intelligence, they are practically inconspicuous. Nevertheless, they are there, and this is something we should know. We would then have to bury once and for all the legend of the weaker sex. Women are not weak. If circumstances demand it, any woman can be as hard, as ruthless, and as rigorous as the chambermaid.

Some Concluding Remarks

I HAVE been dealing with fairy tales for the past thirty years. In 1953, as a young man, I penned an analysis of "Strong Hans" by the Brothers Grimm. And I now felt I had found my mission in life. Enthusiastically, I devoted my time and energy to fairy tales, trying to unveil their secrets and find important psychological insights behind their lovely facades. I suffered a miserable fiasco, a total disaster. The deeper I delved into a fairy tale, the less I understood. The images I was examining began to lead lives of their own, which I could neither influence nor control. Ideas, thoughts, brainstorms whirled through my head. I was helplessly perplexed and far from establishing any order, much less meaning, in my wealth of impressions. I did not have the fairy tales—they had me. I could not get rid of the demons that I had conjured up.

In 1965 I made a second attempt. The result was an essay, "The Second and Third Night in the Fairy Tale 'The Boy Who Set Out to Learn the Meaning of Fear.'" (This was the early version of the discussion of this fairy tale in my book.) But then I had to surrender again to the chaos of notions and sensations that simply overwhelmed me. Instead of continuing my investigations, I sought escape by reading detective stories.

I had personally and painfully experienced the special quality of fairy tales. They are ancient stories. They have survived in popular culture for centuries, wandering from one storyteller to the next, absorbing the wisdom of the people in a dynamic exchange between storytellers and listeners. A process of natural selection allowed only the best fairy tales to survive the passage of time. We still know those tales today, and it is not surprising that children are still fascinated by them. No wonder they got under the skin of an inquisitive young man, who became their thrall. What could I do with the human experiences and elemental feelings concentrated in the images of fairy tales? They exerted a force and a power that I simply could not comprehend, let alone digest. What did I know about life, about people, about passion, about death and destruction? I saw only surfaces. I was furious at the wicked stepmother in "Hansel and Gretel." How can a woman be so inhumane as to cast out her children? I wondered. But this understandable anger prevented me from getting at the heart of the story and at an important insight about things that mothers *have* to do. They simply have to do what every mother bird does: throw their fledglings out of the nest. I made the mistake of identifying with the "poor children." Like them, I didn't want to be tossed out of the warm bed and let go of my mother's apron strings. I was in the story with all my emotions. But I was not above it.

Half a lifetime was to pass until I was able to get beyond a superficial view of fairy tales. I had no easy time of it. It is a difficult job reading fairy tales in a new way, thinking new thoughts and feeling new feelings, forgetting the things that have always been taken for granted. I therefore fled my normal environment. I rented a small, primitive room in an obscure part of town and went there twice a week. Undisturbed, isolated, away from my normal middle-class routine, I lived there with Grimms' fairy tales, a dictionary, paper, and pencils. Here I succeeded at last in escaping the temptation of identifying with the surface emotions. I no longer saw things with the eyes of the fairy-tale heroes and heroines. All at once, I could understand what Hansel and Gretel's mother was thinking. I saw that she was right and that her husband was wrong. Even the proverbially wicked witch appeared in a different light, and the gingerbread house became a symbol of insatiable childhood wishes.

That charming Little Red Riding Hood likewise lost her traditional image and turned into an enterprising and curious girl. And the big, bad, dangerous wolf was no longer a remote and fabled beast. He took on a human personality, which made him real. The scary castle and its eerie ghosts turned out to be vivid metaphors for adolescent crises. And, last but not least, the goose girl, who had once seemed so irritatingly passive, showed that she could act effectively and successfully and get her own way.

Discovering these entirely new perspectives in fairy tales was an exciting, fun-filled adventure. And over and over again, I was stunned to realize how much knowledge about human beings (adults, too, not just children) is contained in fairy tales. Now I could finally write about fairy tales, and I wrote with enormous pleasure. I was helped by the thing that children always like about fairy tales: they almost always have a happy end. This was comforting to me. Fairy tales not only depict problems, they also solve them—even if they have to use a pail of water containing tiny, writhing fish.

Nor is this image covered with historical dust. Most of the images in fairy tales are supermodern, and so are nearly all their big and little protagonists. The famous concluding line of many German fairy tales proved all too true: "And if they haven't died, then they're still alive today!" At the end of this book, I can say: Yes, it's true. Hansel and Gretel, Red Riding Hood, Hans, and the goose girl are our sons and daughters and still a part of the family scene. And even fabled creatures such as the witch and the wolf are not unreal. Who of us doesn't know a wolf, a witch? And who of us doesn't know about the ghosts haunting a magic castle?

When I asked my uncle, the psychiatrist, what children were

all about, he said, "I don't know." And I was furious. Today, I agree with him. I have analyzed only four fairy tales. Yet how different are the children in these four stories! Even Hans and Matthes, although brothers, are worlds apart from one another. And how different are Hansel's sister, Gretel, and Red Riding Hood. Then again, the hybrid goose girl–chambermaid offers an entirely different variety of the female species. And if we recall Snow White and Cinderella, we have completely different sorts of girls. No, *the* child per se does not exist and cannot exist, and that's a good thing. The question "Do you understand children?" cannot be answered.

My good uncle was right in another respect as well. Children are not only different from one another, they are different from what adults may expect or wish them to be. Showing this is the chief aim of my book.

Who would have thought that children hold on so tightly to their mothers' apron strings, they they can be so inventive in defending their childhood privileges as Hansel and Gretel? And wouldn't Red Riding Hood's rescuer, the hunter, have turned beet-red, had he known *why* the little girl drew back the bed curtain? And wouldn't many parents have believed that the little girl meant to keep her promise? Isn't it nice of Hans not to tell anything about his adventures in the haunted castle? Isn't he thereby sparing any number of decent parents? Nor does he talk about his wedding night. The fairy tale, however, reveals everything he goes through. I have no idea what people will say about the goose girl's "magical" strategies. But I do know that I have often fallen victim to very similar feminine wiles.

Even the adults who appear in these fairy tales frequently exhibit a behavior that a child never learns about from his parents or at school. From the sexton, the drayman, and the innkeeper, to the goose girl's two kings, these adults offer a wide range of possible behavior patterns. And as for the fathers and mothers here, one could ask: Do you understand parents?

For me, it was a fascinating world. I spent a long time here, working hard, but always having a good time. Now the last page is written, I have to say goodbye, and I am sorry to be leaving. The heroes and heroines of these four fairy tales have become close friends of mine, and I have also come to respect their wicked adversaries. If I have succeeded in sharing my feelings with my readers, I will be more than satisfied.

Bibliography

T HE various kinds of help that I have gotten from scholarly literature in regard to the nature of children cannot be acknowledged here in detail, for every pertinent book that I have read in the course of many years has contributed to the writing of this book. Along with countless scholarly works—pedagogical, psychological, and psychoanalytical—I was especially helped by fairy tales. Chief among these was the collection put together by the Brothers Grimm, as well as the original version of their stories edited by Friedrich Panzer, published by Emil Vollmer Verlag in Wiesbaden, Germany. I was also influenced by Ludwig Bechstein's fairy tales and by Charles Perrault's tales in German translation.

A few interesting ideas were inspired by Heinrich Hoffmann's *Struwwelpeter* (an English edition of which was published by Routledge and Kegan, 1909), and by *Tom Sawyer* by Mark Twain.

I obtained information on fairy tales from the following: Jacob Grimm, *Deutsche Mythologie*, vol. 1–3 (Graz, Austria: Akademische Druck- und Verlagsanstalt, 1968) [*Teutonic Mythology*, ed. and trans. by James S. Stallybrass (Peter Smith)]; Luigi Santucci, *Das Kind, sein Mythos und sein Märchen* (Hanover: Hermann Schroedel Verlag, 1964); Vilma Mönckeberg, *Das Märchen und unsere Welt* (Düsseldorf: Eugen Diederichs Verlag, 1972); and

the volume *Projekt Deutschunterricht* I (Stuttgart: J. B. Metzlersche
Verlagsbuchhandlung).
I gained some data from Alfred C. Kinsey's *Sexual Behavior in
the Human Female* (Philadelphia: W. B. Saunders, 1953) in German translation.

In regard to the historical aspect of the child and the contents
of fairy tales, I read the German edition of Philippe Ariès, *Centuries of Childhood: A Social History of Family Life* (New York: Vin-
tage Books, 1965), and Jan Hendrik van den Berg, *Metabletica*
(Göttingen: Vandenhoeck & Ruprecht, 1960). Both works offer
interesting conclusions about the nature of children. But neither
these works nor books on cultural history contained any indi-
cations of whether the plots and characters of fairy tales could
be linked to a specific time or place. This confirmed, for me,
the opinion of many scholars of the genre that fairy tales are
timeless and placeless. C. G. Jung and his followers maintain
that fairy tales contain primal images, archetypes, typical situations that people can experience in all periods and cultures. This
may explain both the wide diffusion of fairy tales and their
longevity; at the same time, it allows us to interpret fairy tales
in order to gain universal insights into the character and behavior
of children.

I owe special thanks to the fairy-tale interpretations in Ottokar
Count Wittgenstein's *Märchen, Träume, Schicksale* (Düsseldorf:
Eugen Diederichs Verlag, 1965), as well as the collection *Mär-
chenforschung und Tiefenpsychologie*, edited by Wilhelm Laiblin
(Darmstadt: Wissenschaftliche Buchgesellschaft, 1969). This volume covers the wide spectrum of fairy-tale scholarship; practically all directions are represented, from cultural anthropology
to depth psychology. The following papers in this collection were
a great help to me: Franz Riklin, "Wish Fulfillment and Symbolism in Fairy Tales"; Bruno Jöckel, "Das Reifungserlebnis im
Märchen"; Wilhelm Laiblin, "Das Urbild der Mutter"; Josephine
Bilz, "Menschliche Reifung im Sinnbild." This volume also contains my paper "Analyse des Grimmschen Märchens 'Der starke
Hans' " (first published in 1953 in *Praxis der Kinderpsychologie und*

Kinderpsychiatrie). This was my first attempt at seeing maturation problems and pedagogical aspects in a fairy tale.

It was only when the manuscript of my book was almost finished that I had an opportunity to read Bruno Bettelheim's *The Uses of Enchantment* (New York: Alfred A. Knopf, 1976). I found many germane ideas here and I also took over a few of Bettelheim's thoughts.

Preliminary work for the chapter on "The Boy Who Set Out to Learn Fear" was done by G. Zillinger in his paper "Zur Frage der Angst und der Darstellung psychosexueller Reifungsstufen im 'Märchen vom Gruseln,' " in *Praxis der Kinderpsychologie und Kinderpsychiatrie*, 1963. The same journal (1965) published my "Die zweite und dritte Nacht im Märchen 'Das Gruseln.' " This paper is mentioned in Bruno Bettelheim's book.

Naturally, the use of scholarly literature is indisputable. But I received my most essential inspiration from children themselves, from my experiences with them and their parents, from sharing in their joys as well as their troubles and sorrows.